COINS OF THE POPES

BOOKS BY JOSEPH COFFIN

COIN COLLECTING

OUR AMERICAN MONEY

COINS OF THE POPES

10 LIRE – SILVER   5 LIRE – SILVER

2 LIRE – ACMONITAL   1 LIRA – ACMONITAL

50 CENTESIMI – ACMONITAL   20 CENTESIMI – ACMONITAL

10 CENTESIMI – BRONZE   5 CENTESIMI – BRONZE

COINS
OF THE POPES

By JOSEPH COFFIN

Illustrated with Photographs

COWARD-McCANN, INC.

NEW YORK

18439

Contents

Sixteen pages of illustrations follow the last page of text.

Introduction

COINS OF THE POPES is designed to assist those interested in Papal coins and the history of the Papal States as it is reflected in its coinage. Primarily intended to help collectors who have such coins in their collections, it is hoped that it will also be of interest to those who, while not collectors, still desire to increase their knowledge of the history of the Church.

Thanks are extended to Friar Cosmas Korb, of St. Anthony-on-Hudson, Rensselaer, N. Y., Reverend Samuel Cummings, S. A., of Graymoor, Garrison, N. Y. and to Professor Thomas Ollive Mabbott, Ph.D., Associate Professor of English, Hunter College, New York City, who were of assistance in interpreting the Latin inscriptions on the coins.

Particular thanks are given to Professor Mabbott for his generous assistance. Also to Lee Hewitt, Editor of *The Numismatic Scrapbook Magazine,* Chicago, Ill. for his aid in assembling the photographs.

JOSEPH COFFIN

Coins of the Popes

IT may well be said that the foundation for papal coins was
laid in the early days of the Christian Era. While it is true
that the first papal coins were issued for Pope Adrian I (772–
795) in conformity with the authority given him by the temporal powers to which he had succeeded, and which, through
his friendship with Charlemagne, had been greatly enlarged,
still the first Christian symbols shown on many papal coins go
back to a much earlier period.

The Emperor Constantine the Great really started the use of
Christian symbols on coins in A.D. 312 by showing on the reverse of his coins the labarum, the imperial standard, with a
chrismon, and the inscription *In hoc signo vinces*—"By this
sign thou shalt conquer"—which he saw in the sky surmounting
a cross the night before his great victory.

Later emperors followed Constantine, using the chrismon,
symbols of a cross surmounting a globe, cross on standard, and
others. A lapse occurred when Julian the Apostate (born 331
A.D.) reverted to pagan symbols such as the lion, eagle, croco-
dile, Serapis, and others. But later still other emperors brought
back Christianity and with it the use of Christian symbols, many
of which survive to this day.

The inscription *In hoc signo vinces* used by Constantine the
Great was used again by Pope Julius II (1503–1513) and has
been used frequently on many coins of other Christian rulers.

The Byzantine emperors, or Roman emperors of the East,
continued to use the symbols of Christianity down to the final
decline of the empire with John Zemisces (969–976). Theophania, widow of Romanus II and later the wife of John
Zemisces, is credited with being the first monarch to show the
Blessed Virgin on coins. Still later, after the time of John
Zemisces, it was a common practice of the Holy Roman em-

1

perors and others to use the chrismon, the legend *In Hoc Signo Vinces*, the cross, and other Christian symbols.

The subject of symbols in itself could well take several volumes. In these few paragraphs it is hoped simply to give enough general information to assist the student of the papal coinage and to give in a very brief way the meaning and significance of the early Christian symbols appearing on so many papal coins, as well as on many coins of the Byzantine and Holy Roman Empires. These symbols have in most cases come down to us through the ages and are the same now as they were during the first centuries of the Church.

About the simplest definition of a symbol is that shown in the *Standard Dictionary:* "Something that (not being a portrait) stands for something else; an emblem . . ." But a symbol differs from an emblem in rather an obscure fashion in that an emblem is more a sign of a definite thing. For example, a cross may be used as an emblem of victory, or belief, but it is a symbol of salvation. An effigy of a lion may be an emblem of victory also, but is always, in all lands, a symbol of the ultimate in strength. To put it in simpler form (from the same dictionary), "An *emblem* resembles, a *symbol* represents."

The origin of symbols is submerged in antiquity. They are probably the first attempt at civilization, and the use of the first symbol proved that man had risen a step from the savage. They have been used in all religions and by all races and at all times in historical memory. It is rather a peculiar thing that often the same thing has been used for symbolic purposes in widely separated countries. Thus the Chinese Buddhist symbol of an elephant was used in India and Egypt, the lion has been used by the Egyptians, the Hebrews, and the early Christians, while the Chinese use the fish in temples as a symbol of the all-seeing eye of Buddha and two fish side by side as a symbol of abundance. Religion has given us countless symbols, and these are found in other sects than Christianity. Buddhists, Taoists, Hebrews, Mohammedans, all have their special symbols, and often the symbols are somewhat similar in design if not in meaning. The seven-branched candlestick is a common symbol in both Christianity and Judaism; for the Christian it symbolizes Christ and his church, the light of the world, for the Jew it prefigured the seven gifts of the Holy Ghost or the seven sacraments. It is found on many of the shekels of Judea and Jewish coins.

The first and most important of the Christian symbols is the cross, which is the sign of redemption and salvation and a symbol of faith. There are seven different types of crosses:

1. Latin cross or headed cross (*crux capita*), the ordinary form.

2. Greek cross, consisting of four limbs of equal length.

3. Maltese cross, the badge of the military and religious order of the Knights of Malta, consisting of four triangular limbs of equal length.

4. St. Andrew's cross, shaped like the letter X.

5. Celtic cross, found in ancient Ireland, the arms connected by a circle.

6. Tau cross, resembling a T in shape and named for the Greek letter T.

7. Egyptian cross, the same as the Latin cross, but headed with a ring or handle.

In addition there is the swastika, which is a form of cross, and the double or archiepiscopal cross, used in the arms of patriarchs, archbishops, and bishops.

Among the monograms, one of the most common is the one resembling the letters X and P entwined. This is called the "chrismon" from the Greek letters Chi and Rho, or Ch and R, meaning "Christ" in abbreviated form. The monogram itself is an intriguing study since most of the earlier papal coins showed the Pope's or the Emperor's name in this form.

Animals often appear as symbols. The lamb is a symbol of Jesus Christ; a symbol of innocence and modesty. The lion also symbolized the Saviour, or the evangelist Mark. It is a symbol of solitude and is sometimes shown with pictures of hermit saints. The dragon or a similar monster represents Satan and is an emblem of sin, as is also the serpent, sometimes shown under the feet of the Virgin. However, the serpent shown entwined around a cross is an emblem of the Saviour, recalling the brazen serpent of Moses. An ox is a symbol of Luke.

The fish is a common emblem of the early Christians. It is accounted for by the fact that the Greek word for fish is *ichthus,* which spelled in the old Greek form contained only five letters: I-CH-TH-U-S. These are the first letters of the words "*Iesous Christos, Theou Uios Soter,*" or "Jesus Christ, Son of God, Saviour." The fish is also a symbol of baptism, the apostles, and those who follow the Christian faith.

Flowers and plants are emblems of various things. The olive branch is a symbol of peace and as such dates to a very ancient time. The palm means victory and is often shown with martyr saints. The lily stands for chastity and is shown in pictures of the Virgin, St. Joseph, and other saints. The rose shown on some papal coins is an emblem of beauty and love.

Among the birds, the dove is a sign of the Holy Ghost and is shown on *sede vacante* coins with a few rare exceptions. The Holy Ghost is looked to for guidance, and *sede vacante* coins generally have some short prayer to the Holy Ghost to invoke His aid in selecting a worthy successor to St. Peter. The dove also signifies peace and is shown in this connection on the *sede vacante* coins of 1939, in the arms of the then camerlingo or papal chamberlain, Cardinal Pacelli, later Pope Pius XII. Incidentally, this pope's family name was symbolic of peace, meaning "Peace of Heaven."

The pelican is an emblem of the Redeemer and of the Holy Eucharist. It is shown on papal coins feeding its young with drops of its own blood. There was a legend to the effect that the pelican did feed its young with its blood, hence it is easily seen how this bird came to be a symbol of the Eucharist. An eagle is a symbol of John and is found in pictures of that saint. However, there are instances where papal coins show an eagle as a purely temporal symbol, as on the coins of Innocent XIII with the motto MAGNARVM ALARVM. In this case the eagle was a part of the armorial bearings of the house of Este and is shown at times on coins of Modena, Reggio, and Ferrara, for example on some coins of Duke Ercole I, Cesare II, and others.

A skull denotes meditation and is shown on old coins bearing a figure of St. Jerome. A banner is an emblem of victory; see coins of the Bologna mint showing a lion rampant holding a banner, the city's coat of arms. A chalice surmounted by a Host is another emblem of the Eucharist; a chalice combined with a stole is used to symbolize the holy orders of the priesthood. A crown stands for the power of kings, while a nimbus is shown only on effigies of saints. Pope Urban VIII first promulgated the ruling that only canonized saints may be shown with a nimbus. A ship symbolizes the church, the "bark of St. Peter," and an anchor is an ancient symbol of hope; see the gold scudo of Clement XI, 1706, showing an anchor standing alone on the waves. Crossed keys shown in the popes' arms symbolize the power of the pope, also his divine authority as successor of Peter, who received from Our Lord the "Keys of the Kingdom of Heaven." They are often shown with the tiara or triple crown of the pope, which itself is emblematic of the threefold office of the papacy—teacher, lawmaker, and judge. The coats of arms on many papal coins show the tiara, crossed keys, and, as on coins of Pius IX, shield with two lions; those of Gregory XVI show tiara, crossed keys, and shield with chalice, pelican, hat, and three stars.

Angels are shown with wings denoting swiftness of movement; evangelists are symbolized by four-winged figures, or an ox or an eagle. Saints are often shown with a banner, the emblem of victory, and martyr saints are often depicted on coins or medals with the instrument of their martyrdom, such as St. Andrew's cross, as this saint was said to have died on a cross of this shape. The arrows of St. Sebastian and the gridiron of St. Lawrence are familiar symbols of these saints' martyrdom, and

are frequently pictured with them. Other saints are shown with
symbols showing their work or position, such as the tiara for
popes, miter (double-pointed hat) and staff for bishops, skull
for hermits, and so on.

The Trinity is sometimes shown as a shamrock from its use by
St. Patrick in explaining the Trinity. Also emblematic of the
Trinity is a triangle containing an eye and surmounted by rays,
as shown at the top of the pyramid on the reverse of the Great
Seal of the United States, which appears on the one dollar bills
of this country.

Here are some of the common symbols of saints:

A woman with a lamb—St. Agnes.

A St. Andrew's cross—St. Andrew.

A figure with a tau cross and accompanied by a pig—St. An-
thony.

A knife or an archiepiscopal or processional cross—St. Bartholomew.

A sword or a large wheel—St. Catherine.

A large figure bearing Christ over a river—St. Christopher.

A woman playing a harp or organ—St. Cecilia.

A papal crown or an anchor—St. Clement.

A gridiron—St. Lawrence (or a symbol of faith).

A figure on horseback transfixing a dragon—St. George.

A figure in armor or with a cross slaying a demon or holding
scales—St. Michael, the Archangel.

The monogram IHS on the breast or radiantly in the sky—
St. Ignatius, the founder of the Jesuits (see the issue of Pope
Gregory XIII on the opening of the Jesuit College at Rome).

A figure studying a large open book, or with a staff signifying
a traveling preacher, or with a skull signifying a hermit—St.
Jerome.

A figure with keys and a triple cross, a fish or a cock, or as a
shepherd—St. Peter.

A figure with a lamb at his feet—St. John the Baptist.

A man bound to a tree with his arms tied behind him—St. Sebastian.

A man with a book and a stone in his hand—St. Stephen.

A man armed with a halberd in his hand and a saber at his side—St. Theodore.

As an example of how much symbolism is a part of the study of coins of the popes we might mention two coins in passing which may be studied from the standpoint of symbols alone. These coins, while not common, are by no means rare, and the designers have been more than usually lavish in their display of symbolic figures. They are the silver scudo of Pope Urban VIII (1623–1644) and the silver fifty baiocchi of Pope Gregory XVI (1831–1846).

Taking the scudo of Urban VIII, twelfth year, we note on the reverse St. Michael destroying Satan. The motto reads Vivit Deus—"The Lord Lives." St. Michael in armor is shown with sword and shield, on the latter a cross, a favorite symbol on coins of the popes. Satan is symbolized by a demon, which by a stretch of the imagination could be called a dragon, having the horns, fangs, wings, tail, and hideous countenance of the latter. But the demon shown on this coin is much more human looking (if it were possible for anything so hideous to be called "human looking") than the dragon shown with St. George, which is the distinguishing feature of coins of the popes issued at the Ferrara mint. Another variety of our present coin goes into more detail, showing in vivid manner flames arising from hell, with another demon or lost soul making an effort to arise from the flames while St. Michael is engaged with Satan. Our coin shows a six-pointed star over St. Michael's head, which is missing from the second variety mentioned. The star is generally, with Christians, a symbol of hope, although the pagan Julius Caesar used it to signify his descent from Mars.

The obverse of the fifty baiocchi of Pope Gregory XVI shows his bust to right and the inscription Gregorivs XVI Pont Max

A II—"Gregory XVI, Pontifex Maximus, Second Year." In the exergue is the date, 1832, and in small letters the name N. Cerbara, the engraver.

Pope Gregory XVI, 1831–1846, was born Mauro Cappellari on September 8, 1765, and died in Rome June 9, 1846. He was installed as a novice at the Camaldolesian Monastery of San Michele di Murano in 1783 and professed and ordained a monk in 1787 at Camaldoli, which provides the motif for the reverse of this coin, as we shall see.

Gregory's coat of arms consisted of two pelicans drinking from a chalice, surmounted by a three-leaf clover, and right, a cardinal's hat and three stars. As noted, the pelicans and chalice are symbols of the Holy Eucharist, the three-leaf clover symbolized the Trinity, the stars symbolized Hope.

The reverse of the fifty baiocchi of 1832 shows the legend S. ROMVALDVS AB. CAMAL., with the kneeling saint, his head surrounded by a nimbus or halo, praying with a crucifix in his upraised left hand. His staff is leaning against a rock on which is a skull; in the exergue "Baj. R 50" (the denomination, 50 baiocchi, and "R," mint mark for the Rome mint). The skull is a symbol of the hermit and this picture of the saint praying in a desert scene is symbolic of the life of St. Romuald, while the wooden staff is also symbolic of his wanderings.

St. Romuald was born about 950 and died at Val di Castro in 1027. He became a disciple of St. Apollinaris and later went to Venice and followed under the direction of the hermit Marinus. Henceforth Romuald lived the life of a hermit, in great austerity, wandering through all parts of the country for thirty years. Finally, in 1005, he built a few cells for hermits at Camaldoli, founding the Camaldolesian Order of monks. Thus the inscription "St. Romvaldvs Ab. Camal." or "St. Romuald, Abbot of Camaldoli."

It is self-evident that many of the inscriptions are symbolic, or refer to symbols. For example, Lamb of God, Lion of the

Tribe of Juda, Black but Beautiful, and others. There is one coin that actually has a symbol as its main theme or legend. This is the julio of Gregory XIII, which shows I.H.S.—Cor, purely a symbol of Our Lord's Sacred Heart. This coin was issued in 1582 to commemorate the founding of the Jesuit College of Rome.

It was on a certain foundation, as may well be seen from the preceding pages, that Adrian I started the papal coinage, which has lasted, with, of course, several interruptions of long or short duration, for almost twelve hundred years.

The temporal power of the popes came into being through a grant of a few provinces and towns, made by the Frankish King Pepin to Pope Stephen II. Coinage really started under Pope Gregory III (731–741) and continued under Zacharias (741–752), but these issues are considered as tokens rather than coins and were got out because of a shortage of money in Rome due to continual strife among the papal and civil factions. A regular coinage started with Adrian I, who first issued coins on the authority of Charlemagne, at the beginning following the Byzantine pattern and later adopting the Carlovingian type through the influence of his friend and patron, the great emperor. Charlemagne, after his conquests, had seriously undertaken to reform the very confused and debased coinage system then in vogue, and which had deteriorated after the fall of the Western Empire. Before Charlemagne took to himself the task of setting up a uniform system of coinage, all sorts of debased and almost worthless currency was issued almost at will by each king and often even by minor princes. As the pope's temporal power increased, it was but natural for him to assume the kingly prerogative of coining money.

Silver was used exclusively at first. There are many of the earlier popes after Adrian I who did not leave a single coin. Some may have been struck and lost beyond recovery, although it seems from records of early days that coins were not struck for these popes. Adrian I, who issued the first coins, also used the first inscription of historical significance, VICTORIA DNN. Several popes had very brief tenure and often there were intervals of two or more years between popes. And sometimes there were two and even three claimants to the title. Coins were issued often for the recognized pope and at the same time for the usurper, because of the fact that the latter, generally called antipope, at times had the support of the emperor or the civil authorities. In this study of papal coins, for various reasons, the coins of the antipopes are not mentioned, although Cinagli lists many of them. Another reason for the lack of representation of some popes after Adrian I is the fact that the coins as then issued were fragile and it is possible that in the continuous wars of the Middle Ages many issues were completely lost, or melted down, or even deliberately destroyed by some of the adherents of the pretenders to the papal throne.

The first coins of the popes showed the name of the pope, but often in monogram form, which is hard to decipher at times. Almost always the name of the reigning emperor was also shown, or the name of the city. St. Peter was at first generally shown as protector, later with St. Paul; and finally the bust of the pope or St. Peter came to be used. There were, of course, many developments between the times of Adrian I and our own time. Sede vacante coins were issued first in 1370, between the death of Pope Urban V and the accession of Gregory XI. They are still issued in the same form, the last ones being the silver five and ten lire of 1939, on the death of Pius XI. The papal chamberlain, or camerlingo, takes charge during the interregnum and has the authority to issue sede vacante coins. Most of them follow the same general pattern, obverse the arms of the camerlingo and reverse a reference to the Holy Spirit and a radiant dove. Several cardinals were honored by having their coats of arms as papal chamberlain on three or four separate issues of sede vacante coins as they held office during the pontificates of several popes. A few times the cardinal chamberlain has had his arms shown on sede vacante coins and later has been himself elected pope, the most recent occasion being the present pope, Pius XII, whose arms are shown on the sede vacante coins of 1939.

Another development was the jubilee coins, the first of which Pope Nicholas V issued for the jubilee of 1450. The jubilee issues, like the sede vacante coins, follow a uniform pattern, showing the *Porta Sancta* or Holy Door, sometimes closed and sometimes half torn away, with various figures of angels with trumpets, rays of light, and sometimes an angel above, and the pope with hammer tearing down the door in the presence of the clergy and people. Often the door is shown entirely in place with an angel on either side. The *Porta Sancta* is one of the symbols of the jubilee. The door is previously walled up and the pope on the opening of the jubilee strikes at the bricks and breaks down the door with the singing of hymns and other ceremonies. At the end of the jubilee the door is walled up for another twenty-five years. There are, at times, other special jubilees to commemorate the pope's own jubilee of his priesthood, as some special honor to the Blessed Virgin Mary or to a saint, or for other reasons.

It is probable that this justly famous and most extensive series of coins would be more popular if more collectors were familiar with Latin, which is used exclusively for their legends, mottoes, and inscriptions.

To the writer's mind, these inscriptions are the most fascinating part of the study of papal coins. Some of them are beautiful in expression, others historically interesting, and still others are apt to be puzzling unless the collector has become familiar with their historical significance in the light of the times of the popes during whose pontificates the coins were issued.

The present study is intended to embrace coins only and no medals are included, except insofar as many of the inscriptions may have been duplicated on medals, issued either for the same popes or entirely different ones. As an example, *Tota pulchra es, macula non est in te* is divided into two parts and is shown on separate coins of Popes Innocent XI and Benedict XIV, while in its entirety it has been noted on a medal of Pope Leo XIII, many years later.

The inscriptions shown may be roughly placed in three classifications:

1. Those that refer to scriptural passages, although they may have been chosen particularly in view of passing events as well, such as *Dirige Dne gressus nros* (Lord direct our steps) used by Pope Pius II, and *Exurgat D. et dissipentur inimica ejus* (May God arise and scatter His enemies) on coins of the same pope.

2. Those that are purely prayer or supplication: *S. Maria, Ora pro nobis* (Holy Mary, pray for us), *Ave Gratia Plena* (Hail, full of Grace), and *Virgo Clemens* (Clement Virgin).

3. Inscriptions that might be said to refer to the papacy as an institution, or to the Roman Church, such as *Si Ecclesia Romano,* or to the patron saint of the city in which they were issued, such as *St. Germanius, Mutin.* (Modena), and others.

There is not entire accord, even among Latin scholars, on the exact English equivalent of many of the scriptural passages, and, this being the case, it is natural that there will be some room for argument concerning the versions of one who does not pretend to be a Latin scholar. On the other hand, and luckily, many of the sources of the inscriptions are to be found with the individual words already formed into phrases which are entirely used in a good many of the inscriptions. A little more difficulty is encountered where the inscription has been changed somewhat in form; this often occurs, although the original meaning may have been retained.

The references to numbers for the Psalms and gospels or epistles and scriptural passages are taken from the Douay-Rheims version of the Vulgate. The numbers of the Psalms, on which no two writers seem to agree at times, are those from the Vulgate rather than from the Hebrew version.

As for the meaning behind some of the phrases used, a little study of history would assuredly throw more light on these. Some are easily understood; for example, references to the "Founders of the Church at Rome" and "Possessor of the Holy Lateran Basilica" touch respectively on the apostles and the pope, who, as bishop of Rome, is considered as the possessor of the Lateran Basilica. The latter inscription is found on coins issued for disposition to the faithful upon a pope's taking possession of the Lateran Basilica, the pope's own church, in the early days of his pontificate. These inscriptions are not scriptural, of course, but rather a designation of the authority under which the coins were issued. Similarly, coins of the Bologna mint generally have *Bononia docet,* "Bologna teaches," or some form of this phrase, or *Bononia Mater Studiorem,* "Bologna, Mother of Studies," a reference to the famous University of Bologna, founded early in the thirteenth century. Others, such as "St. Petronius," "St. Ubaldus," "St. Germanius," "St. Herculanus," and "St. George," are shown on coins of Bologna, Gubbio, Modena, Perugia, and Ferrara, respectively, these being the patron saints, or protectors, of those cities in which the coins were minted. SS Peter and Paul are shown as protectors of Rome, with one exception where St. Frances of Rome is mentioned.

A good many of the inscriptions may be explained by an examination of the history of the times of the popes concerned. For example, after the Peace of Ryswick, in 1697, Pope Innocent XII uses the significant and timely legends *Bellum conteram de terra* (I shall destroy war from the earth) and *Loquetur pacem gentibus* (He will speak peace to the nations). The scudo bearing the latter inscription shows a peace council in session. Other popes of the sixteenth and seventeenth centuries, during the troubles of the Reformation, had fitting inscriptions, such as that of Pope Paul III, *Libertas Ecclesiastica* (The Church Liberated); Gregory XIII used *Letamini Gentes* (Rejoice, ye nations).

The Holy Ghost is called upon to bring to a successful conclusion works and deliberations of all kinds and this is reflected in the sede vacante coins of almost all issues for hundreds of years. These vary at times but almost always have some allusion to the Holy Spirit. Thus on sede vacante issues we find such expressions as *Auxilium de Sancto* (Help from the Sanctuary); *Da recta sapere* (May we correctly understand); *Dabitur vobis Paraclitus* (The Holy Spirit will be given you).

Like the designs, the inscriptions on jubilee issues also form a uniform pattern, having some reference to the Porta Sancta, or Holy Door, or to penance, the remission or propitiation of sins during the holy year of jubilee. These consist of such legends as *Clausit Anno Ivbelei* (He closed it in the Year of Jubilee); *Et clavsit* (And he closed it); *Anno Remissionis* (Year of Remission).[1]

Coins may be encountered at times with varying inscriptions not shown on our list in the exact form in which they appear on the coin. This is often due to carelessness on the part of the engraver or die cutter. These instances are numerous and it is not thought necessary to enumerate all of them because their meaning and intent are almost invariably self-evident. Thus on the julio of Pius IV most varieties show correctly SANTV or SANTVS, one shows SATV; on a julio of St. Pius V, GLORIOSI PRINCIPES is shown as GLORIOSI PRINCIES; on a testone of Sixtus V ST. PETRVS is shown as S.PERVS; and so on. Saints and cities are often shown in widely varying form, as on coins of Gregory XIII on which the saint's name appears variously as S.CYRIACVS, S.CIRIA, S.KRIAVS, and S.YRCAVS.

St. George is considered the patron saint of England, and, while this is a well-known fact, it may not be so well known that the same saint is the patron saint of Ferrara and his figure slay-

---

[1] The last Holy Year Jubilee issue appeared on the occasion of the special jubilee of 1933–1934 for Pius XI, for whom there was issued a jubilee set of one hundred lire gold, ten and five lire silver, two and one lire and fifty and twenty centesimi nickel, and ten and five centesimi bronze.

ing the dragon is the distinguishing feature of coins of the Ferrara mint.

St. Petronius is the patron saint of Bologna and his name often is shown on coins of this mint. The conventional design of the reverse of coins of the Bologna mint was a lion rampant, with standard, the arms of the city.

Coins of the Gubbio (old city of Eugubius) mint are often shown with the figure or name of St. Ubaldus, and the mint mark is shown—Evgvbi, Egv, Gvb, or Gvbbio.

Coins of the Rome mint have no distinguishing design but the mint mark is shown as Roma, often separated Ro—Ma with coat of arms between the second and third letters, R, and sometimes Romano, appearing, as a rule, in the exergue.

Some form of the name Ravenna is usually shown on coins of that mint: Raven, Ravennae, Rav, and so on. A cluster of palm branches is shown on the obverse around the pope's coat of arms.

Coins of other mints at which papal coins were issued at times, Fermo, Foligno, Civitavecchia, Spoleto, Terni, Tivoli, Viterbo, Perugia, San Severino, Pergola, Macerata, Matelica, and Montalto, used especially by Pope Pius VI, are shown with the name of the mint in some form or other. This also applies to Avignon, shown as Aven and in other forms, and to Ascoli and Ancona.

The mint at Rome was by far the most prolific in the number and variety of issues. This was to be expected because of its close proximity to the Papal See. Following Rome, Bologna was the major producer of papal coins; a great many sede vacante coins were issued here under the authority of the papal chamberlain. Next in importance was Ferrara, an ancient town which was joined to the Papal States during the pontificate of Pope Clement VIII, who opened a mint at that place, where many fine coins were issued.

Pope Julius II opened the mints at Perugia, Parma, and Reggio for the popes. Sixtus V, who had been a friar at Montalto, upon attaining the papal throne honored the city by establishing a mint there which was used also by his successor, Urban VII.

Pesaro, subject for a short time to the Papal States, issued coins at its mint for Leo X, as did Piacenza.

During the pontificate of Pius VI when Napoleon's armies occupied Rome the Pope was forced to flee from the city and died August 29, 1799, at Valence, in the south of France. The unsettled state of papal affairs during this unhappy period is reflected in the number of places at which papal coins were struck. Coins were issued at no less than ten different mints, among them Fano, Fermo, Foligno, Gubbio, Matelica, Montalto, Pergola, San Severino, Perugia, and Viterbo, in addition to Rome and Bologna.

The new pontiff, Pius VII, again established the seat of the papacy at Rome in 1800 and coins were again issued for the popes at Rome. The Rome mint in the interregnum had been used for the coinage of money of the Roman Republic.

The coins of Piacenza, Parma, Reggio, Modena, and Bologna are closely related. In fact, a glance at a present-day map of Italy will show that these cities stretch on a railroad line almost in a straight line in the order named, from Piacenza, slightly southeast of Milan in the northwest, to Bologna, while on the same line situated on the Adriatic shore is Pesaro, another papal mint city. Continuing on the same railroad along the Adriatic shore we come to Fano and Ancona. Just above Pesaro on the Adriatic is Ravenna and slightly northeast of this city is Ferrara. A short distance southwest of Ancona are Fabriano, Macerata, and Gubbio, then Perugia, Foligno, Spoleto, Terni, Viterbo, and, continuing southwest, Aquila and finally Rome, on the western coast.

Denominations, when shown at all, are easily discernible and should not be puzzling to any collector of papal coins. Benedict XIV was the first pontiff generally to show the denomination.

The most common denominations are *Vn Baiocco* or one baiocco, and later simply *Baiocco; Dve Baiocchi*—two baiocchi;
Mezo or *Mezzo* (half) *Baiocchi; Bolognino; Mezo* or *Mezzo
Bolognino; Cinque* (five) *Bolognini; Vn Carlino, Quattrino*
and *Zecchino; Scudo, Cinque Scudi;* and others less common
such as the julio, scudo d'oro del sol, ducat, madonina, and
testone.

The zecchino is patterned after the French sequin, and comes
from the word *zecca* or "mint."

An unusual denomination is shown on the twenty-five baiocchi piece of Pius VI as *Venticinque Baiocchi.*

In the nineteenth century, beginning in 1869, the denominations followed the pattern of the Italian coins and changed to
soldi, centesimi, and lire.

Coinage for the popes was resumed on the signing of the
Lateran Treaty in 1929 and the establishment of Vatican City.
Coins are issued at only one mint, the Italian mint at Rome,
and the denominations are the same as those issued for Italy,
except that the Pope may issue a limited amount of gold coins,
being one of the few rulers who have that privilege at this time.
Since 1929 coins have been issued for Pope Pius XI, sede vacante 1939 five and ten lire, and for Pope Pius XII in denominations of one hundred lire gold, ten and five lire silver, two and
one lire and fifty and twenty centesimi nickel, and ten and five
centesimi bronze.

In 1942 the nickel coins were discontinued and coinage was
issued in a metal used by the Italian government and called by
it *acmonital,* an alloy of aluminum and steel.

List of Popes

First Century

		Died	
1. St. Peter		67	A.D.
2. St. Linus		78	
3. St. Cletus		90	
4. St. Clement		100	

Second Century

5. St. Anacle	112
6. St. Evaristus	121
7. St. Alexander	132
8. St. Sixtus I	142
9. St. Telesporus	154
10. St. Hyginus	158
11. St. Pius I	167
12. St. Anicetus	175
13. St. Soter	182
14. St. Eleutherius	193
15. St. Victor I	203

Third Century

16. St. Zephyrinus	220
17. St. Calixtus I	227
18. St. Urban I	233
19. St. Pontian	238
20. St. Anterus	239
21. St. Fabian	253
22. St. Cornelius	255
23. St. Lucius I	257
24. St. Stephen I	260

25. St. Sixtus II   261
26. St. Dionysius   272
27. St. Felix I   275
28. St. Eutychian   283
29. St. Caius   296
30. St. Marcellinus   304

Fourth Century

31. St. Marcellus I   309
32. St. Eusebius   311
33. St. Melchiades   314

During his pontificate occurred the great victory of
Constantine the Great, Oct. 3, 312, bringing into use
the first Christian symbols on coins, and the inscription
In hoc signo vinces—"By this sign thou shalt conquer."

34. St. Sylvester I   337
35. St. Marcus   340
36. St. Julius I   352
37. St. Liberius   363

During this period, 361–363, the Emperor Julian the
Apostate reverted to pagan emblems on coins.

38. St. Felix II   365
39. St. Damasus   384
40. St. Siricius   398
41. St. Anastasius I   402

Fifth Century

42. St. Innocent I   417
43. St. Zozimus   418
44. St. Boniface I   423
45. St. Celestine I   432
46. St. Sixtus III   440
47. St. Leo I (the Great)   461

In St. Leo's pontificate occurred (about 450) the death of St. Petronius, Bishop of Bologna, who is honored as protector of the city on coins of the Bologna mint.

48. St. Hilary   468

His name (St. Hilarius) is shown on coins of the Parma mint.

49. St. Simplicius   483

His reign saw the fall of the Western Roman Empire.

50. St. Felix III   492
51. St. Gelasius I   496
52. St. Anastasius II   498

Sixth Century

53. St. Symmachus   514
54. St. Hormisdas   523
55. St. John I   526
56. St. Felix IV   530
57. Boniface II   532
58. John II   535
59. St. Agapitus   536
60. St. Silverius   538
61. Vigilius   555
62. Pelagius I   560
63. John III   573

Birth of Mohammed (570).

64. Benedict I   578
65. Pelagius II   590
66. St. Gregory I (the Great)   604

Seventh Century—Century of the rise of Mohammedanism, which greatly influenced papal coinage in later centuries.

67. Sabinianus 606
68. Boniface III 607
69. St. Boniface IV 615
70. St. Adeodatus I or Deusdedit 619

 Said to be the first pope to use leaden seals or bullae.

71. Boniface V 625
72. Honorius I 638
73. Severinus 640
74. John IV 642

 Mohammedans overran Western Asia, Africa, and Spain, and in 637 occupied Jerusalem.

75. Theodorus I 649
76. St. Martin I 655
77. St. Eugenius I 656
78. St. Vitalian 672
79. Adeodatus II 676
80. Domnus I 678
81. St. Agatho 682
82. St. Leo II 683
83. St. Benedict II 685
84. John V 686
85. Conon 687
86. St. Sergius I 701

Eighth Century

87. John VI 705
88. John VII 707
89. Sisinnius 708
90. Constantine 715
91. St. Gregory II 731
92. St. Gregory III 741

 Issued several tokens used as money during a shortage of coins in Rome.

93. St. Zacharias   752

> During his reign the temporal power of the popes began through a gift of land from the Byzantine Empire, further extended by another grant from the Frankish king Pepin to Stephen II.

94. Stephen II   752
95. Stephen III   757
96. St. Paul I   767
97. Stephen IV   771
98. Adrian I   795

> Issued the first papal coins. A close friend of Charlemagne, he secured for the papal territory the provinces of Venice, Parma, and Istria, the island of Corsica, and the duchies of Spoleto and Benevento. He ruled as pope for twenty-four years, dying on Christmas Day, 795, the length of his pontificate not being exceeded until the death of Pius VI in 1799.

Ninth Century

99. St. Leo III   816

> Crowned Charlemagne emperor.

100. Stephen V   817
101. St. Paschal I   824
102. Eugenius II   827
103. Valentine   827

> Reigned six weeks.

104. Gregory IV   844
105. Sergius II   847

> Said to have been the first pope to change his name.

106. St. Leo VI   855
107. Benedict III   858
108. St. Nicholas I (the Great)   867
109. Adrian II   872

110.	John VIII	882
111.	Marinus I	884
112.	Adrian III	885
113.	Stephen VI	891
114.	Formosus	896
115.	Boniface VI	896
116.	Stephen VII	898
117.	Romanus	898
118.	Theodorus II	898
119.	John IX	900

It will be noted that there were twenty-one popes in this century, five of them in the last five years between 896 and 900. Stephen VII was assassinated in 898; Romanus and Theodorus II died within five months. In that troublous period, the Middle Ages, there were at times two and three claimants to the papal throne simultaneously. Few coins were issued during this century.

Tenth Century

120.	Benedict IV	903
121.	Leo V	903
122.	Christopher	904
123.	Sergius III	911

It is said Leo V was thrown into prison and the papal throne usurped by Christopher, who was in turn ejected by Sergius III, who executed both Leo V and Christopher. Sergius restored the Lateran Basilica, the cathedral church of the pope, as bishop of Rome.

124.	Anastasius III	913
125.	Landus	914
126.	John X	928

Shown on coins as IOH, IOHAN, PA IOS, etc.

127.	Leo VI	929
128.	Stephen VIII	931
129.	John XI	936

Shown on coins as DOM. IOANES PAPA (The Lord John, Pope).

130.	Leo VII	939
131.	Stephen IX	942
132.	Marinus II	946
133.	Agapitus II	956
134.	John XII	964
135.	Benedict V	965
136.	John XIII	972

Zimisces and Theophania, Emperor and Empress of Byzantium (969), first showed the Blessed Virgin on medal and coin.

137.	Benedict VI	973
138.	Domnus II	973
139.	Benedict VII	984
140.	John XIV	985
141.	Boniface VII	985
142.	John XV	996
143.	John XVI	996
144.	Gregory V	999
145.	John XVII	999

The strife and troubles of the ninth century were continued in the tenth, which saw twenty-seven popes and papal claimants. No coins were issued for Leo V, Landus, Leo VI, Leo VII, Stephen IX, Marinus II, Domnus II, John XV, John XVI, Gregory V, or John XVII.

Eleventh Century

| 146. | Sylvester II | 1003 |
| 147. | John XVIII | 1003 |

148. John XIX	1009
149. Sergius IV	1012
150. Benedict VIII	1024
151. John XX	1033
152. Benedict IX	1044
153. Gregory VI	1046
Resigned.	
154. Clement II	1047
155. Damasus II	1048
156. St. Leo IX	1054
157. Victor II	1057
158. Stephen X	1058
Reigned eight months.	
159. Benedict X	1059
160. Nicholas II	1061
161. Alexander II	1073
162. St. Gregory VII	1085
163. Victor III	1087
164. Urban II	1099

Of the eighteen popes in this century only John XIX, Sergius IV, St. Leo IX, and Benedict X are known to have had coins issued.[1]

---

[1] The Right Rev. Horace K. Mann, in *The Lives of the Popes in the Middle Ages*, Vol. IV, Kegan Paul, Trench, Trubner & Co., Ltd., London, and B. Herder Book Co., St. Louis, Mo., 1925, writes (on Gregory V): ". . . we have to regret that the light, small but clear, which numismatology has hitherto so often furnished us, will fail us almost entirely for three centuries, viz., for the Eleventh, Twelfth and Thirteenth. Not accepting as belonging to Philagathus the coins which Cinagli assigns to him, Promis contends that, with the exception of those of St. Leo IX and Paschal II (1099–1118) no papal coins are extant from the days of Benedict VII (975–983) to those of Blessed Benedict XI (1301–1305). Pizzamiglio, however, shows good reason for holding that coins which Promis assigns to Benedict VII and Sergius III of the Tenth Century really belong to Benedict VIII and Sergius IV of the Eleventh Century. Still, even if his contention be allowed, papal coins will not supply us with much material for the next 300 years."

Twelfth Century

165.	Paschal II	1118

From the death of Urban II (1099) to the pontificate of Benedict XI (1303), coins were issued under the Senate of Rome, generally shown with some form of the legend *Roma Caput Mundi—S.P.Q.R.* (Rome Capital of the World—The Senate and the Roman People). This legend also appears on coins of Martin V (died 1431).

166.	Gelasius II	1118
167.	Calixtus II	1124
168.	Honorius II	1130
169.	Innocent II	1143
170.	Celestine II	1144
171.	Lucius II	1145
172.	Eugenius III	1153
173.	Anastasius IV	1154
174.	Adrian IV	1159
175.	Alexander III	1181
176.	Lucius III	1185
177.	Urban III	1187
178.	Gregory VIII	1187

Reigned two months.

179.	Clement III	1191
180.	Celestine III	1198
181.	Innocent III	1216

Thirteenth Century

182.	Honorius III	1227

Founding of university at Piacenza.

183.	Gregory IX	1241
184.	Celestine IV	1241
185.	Innocent IV	1254

186. Alexander IV   1261
187. Urban IV   1264
       Founding of university at Ferrara.

188. Clement IV   1269
189. Gregory X   1276
190. Innocent V   1276
       Reigned five months.

191. Adrian V   1277
       Reigned five weeks.

192. John XXI   1277
193. Nicholas III   1280
194. Martin IV   1285
195. Honorius IV   1287
196. Nicholas IV   1292
197. St. Celestine V   1296
       Resigned.

None of these popes issued any coins.

198. Boniface VIII   1303
       Coinage of popes resumed. First jubilee held 1300.

Fourteenth Century

199. Benedict XI   1304
200. Clement V   1314
       At Avignon.

201. John XXII   1334
       At Avignon.

202. Benedict XII   1342
       At Avignon.

203. Clement VI   1352

At Avignon. Issued coins at Avignon, designated *Comes Venesi* or *Comes Venaisin,* from the Comte Venaisin district of France.

204. Innocent VI   1362

   At Avignon.

205. Blessed Urban V   1370

   At Avignon. Beginning of coinage for the popes at the Bologna mint. The university was founded in this city late in the thirteenth century and is commemorated on Bolognese coinage by the legends *Bononia Docet* (Bologna Teaches) and *Bononia Mater Studiorum* (Bologna, Mother of Studies).
   First sede vacante coins were issued.

206. Gregory XI   1378

   See restored to Rome.

207. Urban VI   1389

Fifteenth Century

208. Boniface IX   1404

   First coins of Macerata mint.

209. Innocent VII   1406
210. Gregory XII   1415

   Resigned.

211. Alexander V   1420
212. John XXIII   1422

   Resigned.

213. Martin V   1431

   First modern papal medal.

214. Eugenius IV   1447
215. Nicholas V   1455

   First coins of Foligno mint and the first jubilee coins.

216. Calixtus III   1458
217. Pius II   1464

> Issued Provincia Ducat. Inscription: Pɪɪ—PP II Pon A
> IIII (Pius, Pater Patrium II Pontiff, Anno 1111—fourth
> year of pontificate).

218. Paul II   1471
219. Sixtus IV   1484

> First jubilee coin with inscription: S. Pavlvs—S. Petrvs
> An Ivbile (St. Paul—St. Peter—Year of Jubilee).

220. Innocent VIII   1492

> First coin issued for popes at Aquila.

221. Alexander VI   1503

> First coins issued for popes at Ferrara. Alexander VI is
> supposed to have originated the ceremonies of the Porta
> Sancta or Holy Door in jubilee years.

Sixteenth Century

222. Pius III   1503

> Reigned only twenty-six days, but there is one coin read-
> ing Pɪus Papa Tertivs (Pope Pius III). It was com-
> mon in early days to show titles thus—Pius Primus (Pius
> I), Pius Secundus (Pius II), Pius Quartus (Pius IV), and
> so on.

223. Julius II   1513

> Did much to modernize the coinage.

224. Leo X   1521

> A member of the Medici family and a lover of the fine
> arts, which he greatly enhanced by employing the most
> gifted artists and engravers.

225. Adrian VI   1523
226. Clement VII   1534

> Issued gold scudi.

227. Paul III   1549
228. Julius III   1555
229. Marcellus II   1555
> Reigned twenty-two days.

230. Paul IV   1559
231. Pius IV   1565
232. St. Pius V   1572
> The great victory over the Turks at Lepanto occurred during his pontificate.

233. Gregory XIII   1585
234. Sixtus V   1590
> Issued first scudo of silver—then called *piastre*.

235. Urban VII   1590
> Reigned thirteen days.

236. Gregory XIV   1591
237. Innocent IX   1592
238. Clement VIII   1605

Seventeenth Century

239. Leo XI   1605
> A member of the Medici family (Cardinal Alessandra Ottaviona de Medici). Reigned twenty-seven days.

240. Paul V   1621
> Coins of Ferrara, half grosso, show on obverse PAVLVS V BVRGHESIVS, reverse FERRARIAE. Others show PAVLVS V and BURGH PONT MAX or BVRGHESIVS P. M. A. ROMA. One grosso shows obverse PAVLVS V BVRGHESIVS and reverse PAVLVS V BVRGHESIVS P. M.; one has both obverse and reverse PAVLVS V PONT MAX. Paul V was born Camillo Borghesi. In two other instances the family

name of the pope is used this way, on coins of Paul's
successor Gregory XV and on those of Urban VIII.[1]

241. Gregory XV   1623

On coins of Ferrara, quattrino and half baiocco, Gregory
XV is designated with his family name, thus: GREGORIVS
XV LVDOVISIVS P. MAX. Before his election he was
Cardinal Alessandro Ludovisi.

242. Urban VIII   1644

On coins of Ferrara, quattrino and half baiocco, he is
shown as VRBANVS VIII BARBERINVS—PONT. M. or P. M.
Before election Urban VIII was Cardinal Maffeo Barberini.[2]

243. Innocent X   1655

First scudo showing pope with tiara.

244. Alexander VII   1667
245. Clement IX   1669
246. Clement X   1676
247. Innocent XI   1689
248. Alexander VIII   1691
249. Innocent XII   1700

In 1700 there were three separate issues of jubilee coins—for
Innocent XII, sede vacante, and for Clement XI. Innocent XII
opened the Holy Door, Clement closed it; both issued jubilee
coins, as did Cardinal Spinola, the papal camerlingo during the
interregnum.

[1] Clement VII (Giulio de Medici) has his family name shown on the quattrino
of Leo X as IVL CAR. MEDICES (Julius, Cardinal Medici).

[2] Not to be confused with the gold quattro scudi of 1629 and other years reading FRANCISCVS CARD. BARBERINVS LEG AVEN, which refer to Cardinal Francisco
Barberini, papal legate at Avignon 1623–1633, and the same denomination of
1634 and later reading ANTONIVS CARD. BARBERINVS LEGAT AVEN, referring to Cardinal Antonio Barberini, papal legate at Avignon 1633–1644. Both of these men
were nephews of Urban VIII. Similarly, the scudi of 1618 issued at Avignon
inscribed SCIP BVRGHESIVS CARD. LEG. AVEN. were for Cardinal Scipione Borghesi,
a relative of Paul V.

Eighteenth Century

250. Clement XI   1721

> First showed denomination—*Mezo* (*Mezzo*) *Baiocco,* etc.

251. Innocent XIII   1724
252. Benedict XIII   1730

> First showed denomination of zecchino—1729. *Zecchino*
> is said by some to come from the French *sequin,* but
> more probably is derived from the Italian *zecca,* "mint."

253. Clement XII   1740
254. Benedict XIV   1758
255. Clement XIII   1769
256. Clement XIV   1774
257. Pius VI   1799

> In 1798 the French Republic operated the mint at Rome,
> and it was out of papal hands until 1814. This pope
> issued coins at many mints outside Rome during the
> Napoleonic Wars. Pius VI fled from Rome in 1797.

Nineteenth Century

258. Pius VII   1823

> In 1800 Pius VII returned to Rome.

259. Leo XII   1829
260. Pius VIII   1830

> Reigned one year.

261. Gregory XVI   1846
262. Pius IX   1878

> Reigned thirty-two years, the longest of any pope. The
> Roman Republic took over the pope's privilege of coin-
> ing money in 1849, but coinage was soon resumed until
> 1869, when it ceased entirely except for one or two pat-
> tern coins. No jubilee was held in 1850 and none in
> 1875. The coinage was reformed and patterned after the

Italian—lire, soldi, and centesimi—in 1866. The last papal issue occurred in 1870, not to be resumed until 1929.

263. Leo XIII   1903

No coins were issued but a pattern five lire piece was struck (by French friends of the papacy, according to some authorities). This coin, however, never became current.

Twentieth Century

264. Pius X   1914

No coins.

265. Benedict XV   1922

No coins.

266. Pius XI   1939

Lateran Agreement arranged, 1929. Papal coinage resumed, 1929. Since that time there have been coins for Pius XI, sede vacante 1939, and for Pius XII, all issued at the Italian mint in Rome.

267. Pius XII

Papal Mints

"M. M." in this list is used as an abbreviation for "Mint marks or distinguishing characteristics." The asterisk (*) denotes places at which papal coins were minted during the pontificate of but one, two, or three popes, at times under contract to these state mints; at other times, as during the pontificate of Pius VI, some of these places minted papal coins because the papal authority was threatened by troubles at Rome when the French, in the course of the Napoleonic Wars, occupied Rome. Some state mints, as those at Reggio, Modena, Parma, Pesaro, and Piacenza, issued papal coins because the territories in which they were located were taken over for the pope by force of arms.

Ancona

Sixtus IV (1471–1484), and at intervals to Pius VI (1775–1799).

M. M.: ANCON; ANCONA; A. D. or C. F. (*Ancon Dorica, Civitas Fidei*). One issue is inscribed SIGN. PRISCAE ANCON—ancient seal of Ancona. St. Peter (S. Petrus) is often mentioned on coins of Ancona and the Marches.

* Aquila

1484 for Innocent VIII, "*Regno di Napoli.*" M. M.: Aquilana.

Ascoli

At intervals from Martin V (1417–1431) to Alexander VI (1492–1503) and to Pius VI (1775–1799) and sede vacante 1799—Rome Republic 1799.

M. M.: DE ASCVLO.

Avignon (France)

Clement V (1305–1314) to Innocent XII (1691–1700) at intervals. The popes resided in Avignon from the pontificate of Clement V through that of Urban V (1362–1370). Gregory XI (1370–1378) restored the See to Rome. Coins continued to be issued at Avignon, however, generally with the name of the cardinal legate.

M. M.: AVE; AVEN; AVENIONEN; etc. Some are marked by the legend *Comes Venasi* or *Comes Venaisin*.

Bologna

While not the oldest papal mint, Bologna, after Rome, was the most important.

Coinage began under King Enrico VI in 1191 and the mint operated until 1861, 670 years. The mint came under the jurisdiction of the popes with Innocent VI from 1360 to 1362, a short time after the famous university was established in the city. However, it was not until 1362, under Blessed Urban V (1362–1370), that coins were issued for the pope, the first denomination being the bolognino.

Gregory XI (1370–1378) continued operation until 1376, when the Republic took charge until 1401. The motto *Bononia Docet,* "Bologna Teaches," a reference to the university, first appeared on the bolognino of the Republic during this period, as did the other most favored inscription, *Bononia Mater Studi-(orum)*—"Bologna, Mother of Studies."

In 1401 the first Lord Giovanni Bentivoglio seized the city but it was regained the following year by Lord Giangaleazzo Visconti, Duke of Milan. Coins of the popes were again minted for Alexander V in 1409 and 1410 and, following him, John XXIII (1410–1415) and with the restoration of Bologna to the church under Martin V (1417–1431), coinage was regularly resumed until 1438. In this year Bologna came under the domination of Filippo Maria, Duke of Milan. In 1443 the Bentivoglio family regained control, followed by the Republic. Pope Pius II (1458–1464) issued coins from this mint, as did Paul II (1464–1471), Sixtus IV (1471–1484), Innocent VIII (1484–1492), and Alexander VI (1492–1503), all showing S. PETRVS APOSTOLVS or BONONIA DOCET or both. Julius II (1503–1513) shows the first deviation in legends with BON. P. IVL-A-TIRANO LIBERAT. Leo X (1513–1521) also used the mint. Clement VII (1523–1534) issued coins at Bologna with the legend COGENTE INOPIA REI FRVMENTARIAE on a ten ducat and three ducat piece, referring to the sack of Rome in 1527, and later coined a half scudo and double julio with the same motto.

Paul III, Julius III, Marcellus II, Paul IV, Pius IV, St. Pius V, and Gregory XIII all had issues at this mint, with only the last named deviating from the legends *Bononia Docet, Bononia Mater Studiorum,* and *S. Petrvs Apostolvs.* He used the legend *Bononia Praeclara Studiorum Alumna* on a silver scudo of the eighth year of his papacy, *Levata Onere Patria* on a scudo of the same year, 1579, and *Hinc Fides et Fortitudo.* The latter legend was continued in use by Sixtus V (1585–1590) on scudi and testones. No further changes in mottoes appear until 1611 (Paul V), when a quattrino shows *Ave Maria.*

Sixteen-twenty under Pope Paul V marks the first use of the inscription honoring the Blessed Virgin Mary, *Praesidium et Decus* (A Protection and Adornment), which inscription was used with regularity to and including the coins of the Republic, 1796–1797, although during the eighteenth century it was not used by Benedict XIII (1724–1730) and Clement XII (1730–1740).

On the sede vacante coinage of 1691 Cardinal Altieri showed the motto *Da Recta Sapere.* In the seventeenth and early eighteenth centuries, coins were issued for practically all popes, from Paul V (1605–1621) to Clement XI (1700–1721), as well as for sede vacante periods. During the eighteenth century Cardinal Annabile Albani issued sede vacante coins for 1721, 1724, 1730, and 1740, one of the few instances where the cardinal chamberlain had the privilege more than once or twice.

Benedict XIV (1740–1758) used several new mottoes: Pastori et Principi Senatus Bononiensis, Patri Patriæ, Vnvm Omnivm Votvm Salvs Principis, and Patrie et Scientarivm Institvto Magnifice Aucto SPQB. These are all explained under "Inscriptions."

Pius VI (1775–1799) issued zecchini, scudi, and half scudi with the motto Adventvs Optimi Principis, at Bologna.

Coinage at Bologna changed with the Republic in 1796–1797, although *Praesidium et Decus* was still used, with other added legends.

The Bologna mint came under the domination of Napoleon I, Emperor of France and King of Italy, from 1809 to 1814, and coins issued there read *Napoleone Imperatore e Re* and *Regno d'Italia*.

After the pontificate of Pius VI *Bononia Docet* and *Bononia Mater Studiorum* do not appear on coins, and the mint at Bologna is identified merely by the mint mark "B."

Pius VII (1815–1823) again used the mint at Bologna. His doppia showed the legend Princeps Apostol. and the grosso Pavperi Porrige Manvm Tvam, and the scudo and half julio Auxilium de Sancto.

On the death of Pius VII the sede vacante coins of Bologna, 1823, showed Princeps Apostolorvm and Auxilium. Leo XII also used these mottoes, as did Cardinal Francesci Galeffi on sede vacante coins of 1829.

Pius VIII (1829–1830) used only one new inscription (he reigned one year): Isti Svnt Patres Tvi Veriqve Pastores. Coins were issued for sede vacante 1830–1831 with Veni Lumen Cordium on a scudo and testone. Gregory XVI (1831–1846) issued a scudo with the same motto, and a fifty baiocchi with S. Romvaldos Ab. Camal and a doppia with Tvrem Tvere Pvblicam.

Pius IX issued coins at Bologna from 1846 to 1848, after which the Rome Republic operated the mint until 1849, when Pius IX again controlled the operation until 1859, at which time it passed entirely from the hands of the popes to King Vittorio Emanuele II.

St. Petronius was the patron saint of Bologna and coins are generally found with "*S. Petronius Prot.*," honoring him as the protector of the city.

Camerino

Coins were issued at this mint for Leo X (1513–1521), Clement VII (1523–1534), Paul III (1534–1549), and Clement X (1670–1676). M. M.: CA; CAM; CAMER; CAMERS; CAMERINI. Coins are generally inscribed to St. Paul.

* Carpentrasso

Coins of Clement VIII (1592–1605).
M. M.: CARPEN.

* Civitavecchia

Civitavecchia was one of the ports of Rome, the ancient Centumcellae. Many popes were greatly interested in enlarging the port facilities, and a picture of the harbor is featured on the silver scudo, dated 1672, of Pope Clement X.

Pius VI (1775–1799) issued some coins at Civitavecchia.

* Patrimonia di S. Pietro

The Patrimony of St. Peter was a part of the Papal States.
Coins were issued here by Benedict XI, John XXII, and Benedict XII.

* Comitato

Coins of Boniface VIII (1294–1303).

Fermo

Coins of Boniface IX (1389–1404) and at intervals until Pius VI (1775–1799).

Ferrara

Coinage at the Ferrara mint started for the dukes d'Este in the twelfth century. The first papal coins issued at Ferrara were coined for Clement VIII (1598–1605), and similar coins (testones) were minted by Paul V (1605–1627). Coins were thereafter issued at intervals, for sede vacante 1621, Gregory XV (1621–1623), sede vacante 1623, Urban VIII (1623–1644), Innocent X (1644–1655), and, with the exceptions of Clement IX, Alexander VIII, Innocent XII, Benedict XIII, and Clement XII, for all popes to Benedict XIV, at whose death in 1758 the mint was closed.

Coins of Ferrara are identified by a figure of St. George slaying the dragon or by a reference to St. George as protector of the city, or to St. George and St. Maurelius.

M. M.: FERRARIAE; DE FERRARIAE.

Fuligno

Eugene IV (1431–1447), and at intervals to Pius VI (1775–1799).

M. M.: FULGIN; FVLG; FVLGINIA.

Coins show S. FELICIANVS DE FVLGINIA to honor St. Felicianus as protector of the city.

* Fabriano

Coins of Leo X (1513–1521).

Fano

Leo X (1513–1521), and at intervals to Pius VI (1775–1799).

M. M.: FANVM FORTVNAE[1]; FANVM FORTV; CIVITAS FANI; S. PATERN FANVM or S. PATERNIANI—FANI, for the patron saint of the city.

---

[1] Fanum Fortunæ was the ancient name of the city; the name means "Temple of Fortune," and this was the site of Julius Caesar's Temple of Fortune.

Gubbio

Gubbio, the ancient town of Eugebius, was the site of the mint from which many thousands of copper coins from the pontificate of Innocent X (1644–1655) emanated, and copper coins in great profusion were issued at Gubbio for the following popes: Alexander VII (1655–1667), Clement IX (1667–1669), Clement X (1670–1676), Innocent XI (1676–1689), Innocent XII (1691–1700), and several others down to Pius VI (1775–1799).

M. M.: Gubbio; Gvb; Evg; Evgebivs; etc.

The patron saint and protector of the city was St. Ubaldus, who is usually shown S. Vbaldvs, San Vbaldvs, or S. Vbaldvs Epis (copus). SS Peter and Paul are occasionally shown.

Macerata

Boniface IX (1389–1404) to Rome Republic, 1798, at intervals.

M. M.: S. Ivlia or S. Ivli Macer; S. Ivlianvs Macer.

Saints usually shown as protectors: St. Peter (S. Petrvs Macerata), St. Syriacus (S. Qviriacvs, S. Kiriacvs, S. Ki), St. Julian (S. Ivli, S. Ivlianvs, etc.). (Feast days: St. Cyriacus, August 8; St. Julian, January 9.)

The Marches

Boniface IX (1389–1404) to Paul II (1464).

M. M.: Marchia; Marcia; Marc; etc.

Coins generally show S. Petrvs de Marcha.

* Matelica

Coins of Pius VI (1775–1799).

Modena

The first record of the Modena mint is dated 1226. Its first coinage was for Emperor Frederick II, 1242. The principal coinage of the mint, however, was for the dukes d'Este of Modena and Ferrara in the fifteenth and sixteenth centuries. Ercole I of the Este family issued coins here, as did Alfonso I, his son, the second husband of Lucrezia Borgia, a member of the family of Alexander VI[1].

In 1510 Modena was occupied by the forces of Julius II under the Roman emperor Maximilian, who issued coins at the Modena mint. Pope Leo X issued ducats and Adrian VI issued some minor coins, which coinage was continued in sede vacante 1523. Clement VII coined some ducati d'oro and quattrini until his imprisonment in the Castle Sant' Angelo in 1527 during the sack of Rome, during which period Modena was reoccupied by Alfonse II of the Este family and coinage ceased for the popes but continued for the various dukes d'Este, Ercole II, Alfonse II, Cesare, Alfonse III, Francesco I, Alfonse IV, and, under the regency of the Duchess Laura, Francesco II and Duke Rinaldo. Louis XIV of France issued coins at Modena in 1705. Duke Rinaldo returned to the city in 1706 and issued coins at the mint, as did his successors until the last record of the mint's existence in 1795.

It will be noted that the Papal States came into the history of the Modena mint for only eighteen years, beginning with Julius II, 1510, followed by Leo X, Adrian VI, sede vacante 1523, and ending with Clement VII in 1527.

Coins of Modena, Parma, Piacenza, and Reggio are closely associated with the noble family of the dukes d'Este of Modena and Ferrara and only appear in the record of papal money during the first part of the sixteenth century, as shown.

St. Geminianus was the protector or patron saint of Modena and is shown in various forms.

M. M.: Mvt; Mvtin; Mvtinensis; etc.

[1] Calixtus III (Alfonso de Borgia) was also a member of this family, as was St. Francis Borgia.

* Montalto

Coins for Julius II, Sixtus V, Urban VII, sede vacante 1590, and Pius VI.

M. M.: MONT ALTO; MONTE ALTO; etc.

* Orvieto

Coins for Julius II (1503–1513).

Parma

Parma has the distinction of having issued coins for Charlemagne (773–800). Coinage began about the year 781 with a denarius for Charlemagne with the legend CAROLVS and the letters PRAM and a later denarius with CAROLVS and PARM. The next record of coinage shows a denarius for Conrad about 1027 —CONRADVS AVGVS on obverse and CIVITAS PARMA on reverse. Coins were issued for King Philip (1207–1208), Otto IV (1208–1209), and Frederico II (1220–1250), who coined the first issue of any account. Following him the Republic issued coins at Parma to the year 1322. The first mention of Hilarius, the patron saint and protector of the city, appears on a grosso of the Republic about 1269, as S. YLARIVS. The first papal coinage at Parma was issued from 1322 to 1329 for John XXII, who issued half grossi with the inscription PP IOHES XXII on obverse and ECCLIE ROME on reverse and later a denarius with the same design and legend.

Later coins were issued for John, King of Bohemia, Guido, Lord of Correggio, and various lords of Parma.

Julius II took possession of the city 1512–1513 and issued ducats inscribed IVL II PON MA MVNVS on obverse and VIRGO FAVEAS PARMAE TVAE, a plea to the Blessed Virgin for aid.

The mint was operated from 1513 to 1515 and again in 1521 for Leo X, who included St. John with St. Hilary: S. HILARIVS—S. IOHES; he also used the motto ECCE AGNVS DEI (Behold the Lamb of God).

On the death of Pope Leo X coins were issued at Parma for Adrian VI in 1522 and 1523, and the pope continued to issue money at this mint even with the return of Lord Francesco I to Parma. The inscriptions now used were DOMINVS PARMAE; VRBIS PARMÆ SECVRITAS; S. ROMANA ECCLESIA; RESTITVTA AVREA PARMA; DIVO THOME; DIVO THOM; and SANCTVS THOMAS. In order these are: "The Lord of Parma"; "Security of the City of Parma"; "The Holy Roman Church"; "Golden Parma Restored"; and three references to St. Thomas.

Paul III issued coins at Parma with some of these legends, and coins were also issued during the interregnum 1523, inscribed S. ROMANA ECCLESIA and S. IONNES—S. HILARIVS (St. John—St. Hilary). Clement VII (1523–1534) used the inscription VERA REDEMPTIO—FIDA PROTECTIO: "Truth redeems—Faith protects"; and ECCE FIDES (Behold faith), with reverse SVB TVVM PRAESIDIVM (Under thy protection), in honor of the Blessed Virgin.

Paul III from 1534 to 1545 used a new legend on coins from the Parma mint with HAEC QVAE ATTVLIT SALVTEM (This which bears salvation).

Coinage continued at the Parma mint under the Farnese family, an old Roman family, one member of which, Cardinal Alexander Farnese, became Pope Paul III (1534–1549), until the end of the seventeenth century, and was operated for various other rulers through the eighteenth century. Operations were suspended during the Napoleonic Wars from 1802 to 1804, but were resumed later and continued intermittently, the last record being the coinage of a twenty-five lire and a proof five lire for the first Lord Roberto di Borbone (1854–1859).

M. M.: PARMEN; PARMA; PARMAE; etc.

Patron saint: St. Hilary, shown HILARIVS, etc., and sometimes with St. John—S. IONNES. (Feast days: St. Hilary, January 14; St. John the Baptist, August 29.)

* Pergola

Coins were issued at this mint for Pius VI (1775–1799).

Perugia

At intervals from Julius II (1503–1513) to the Roman Republic, 1798.

M. M.: Avgvsta Pervsia.

* Pesaro

Leo X (1513–1521).

M. M.: Adte Pisarvm (To you, Pesaro).

* Piacenza

Coinage started at Piacenza in the twelfth century. Conrad II (1240–1313) issued a few coins at this city, as did other rulers until the beginning of the sixteenth century. The city and mint came under the domination of the popes with Julius II, 1503–1513. Leo X issued some coins at Piacenza from 1514 to 1516, as did Adrian VI in 1522 and 1523. The legend mentioned in the list of inscriptions, Ad Patria Redii, used by Adrian VI, appeared on coins of this mint. Coins were issued during sede vacante 1523 and for Clement VII (1523–1534). Paul III also used the mint at Piacenza, using a new inscription —Non Alivnde Salvs. Following Paul III the city reverted to the Farnese family, as did Parma.

Ravenna

Ravenna was one of the oldest of the papal mints, preceded only by Rome. Operations began in 476 and continued at intervals for various rulers and for several popes until the death of Pope Benedict XIV in 1758, or for a period of 1,282 years.

Coins of the Roman Empire were produced here from the opening, practically continuously to and including Charlemagne, from about 770 to 781. After Charlemagne no coins of

which any record can be found were minted here until the
thirteenth century. The Republic of Venice used the mint
from 1440 to 1509. The city was taken by the forces of Leo X,
who from 1517 to 1521 issued several varieties of coins including zecchini, julios, half julios, and quattrini. The first
ducats were struck by Longinus, governor of Italy, who pro-
claimed himself Duke of Ravenna.[1]

Paul III (1534–1549) issued a testone at Ravenna with the
motto Tv Avtem Idem Ipse Es.

Cinagli attributes the julio and grosso of Clement XII reading respectively Esavrientes Implebo and Tolle et Proiice to
Ravenna. However, it is questionable whether there was any
coinage for this pope at Ravenna. *Corpus Nummorum Italicorum* attributes the two coins mentioned to the Rome mint.

Pope Benedict XIV in 1740, 1744, and 1745 issued several
quattrini and mezzo (half) baiocchi at Ravenna, and also issued
coins here in 1746, 1747, and 1750. In the last mentioned year
some jubilee quattrini and half baiocchi were issued for this
pope at Ravenna.

M. M.: Ra.; Rav.; Rave.; Ravenne; or Ravennae Antiqve.
The later coins of this mint are also identified by a palm around
the arms of the pope.

St. Apollinaris is mentioned as the patron saint of Ravenna
and is shown S. Apolinarivs, S. Ap, and Sapol. (Feast day
July 23.)

* Recanati

Nicholas V (1447–1455).

* Reggio

Coinage began at this mint in 1233 and continued later under
the various dukes d'Este.

The mint was operated by Pope Julius II in 1512, 1513, and
1514, who issued coins inscribed Ivlivs II P. M. Regivm Lepidi

---

[1] Ducat was the name given to a coin struck in the domains of a duke.

or REGIVM OLIM AEMILIA. Leo X and Adrian VI also issued coins with the same inscriptions. The mint reverted to Alfonso I of the Este family, and was operated until 1573.

Rome

The mint at Rome was in operation during the time of the old Roman Empire. After the fall of the Western Empire the mint continued coining money for the barbaric kings and for the Byzantine emperor, or Roman emperor of the East.

The first papal coins, issued by Adrian I, were minted at Rome, according to most authorities, although, from the fact that the first denaro of this pope has the letters CONOB., it is thought that these coins may have been struck at Constantinople.

The mint was operated by the Roman Senate for some time from the ninth to the eleventh centuries and for most of the twelfth. Late in the twelfth century under Clement III the mint was again placed in charge of the pope. With the permission of the Senate the popes continued to issue coins until the fifteenth century, mostly in denominations of denari, piccioli, grossi, gold zecchini, and ducati di camera, or gold florins.

Pope Eugene IV rebuilt the mint and placed it near the Vatican. It was later moved several times, the last time by Alexander VII, who placed it in the Vatican Gardens, where it remained until 1911.

It was at the Rome mint that most of the famous engravers worked, among them Cellini, the Hamerani, St. Urbain, the Borners, Kornmann, and many others.

Since 1929 the coins of Vatican City have been issued at the Italian mint at Rome under an agreement with the Italian government.

M. M.: R.; RO; ROMA, ROMANO; etc.

Protectors: SS Peter and Paul.

* San Severino

Pius VI (1775–1799) issued coins at San Severino in denominations of quattrino, half baiocco, two and one-half baiocchi, and five baiocchi.

M. M.: S. SEVERI; S. SEVERINO; SAN SEVERINO.

* Spoleto

Julius II (1503–1513) and Pius VI (1797).
M. M.: SPOLETVM.

* Terni

Pius VI (1797).

* Tivoli

Pius VI (1797).

* Viterbo

Urban VI (1378), Sixtus IV (1471), Pius VI (1797). The sede vacante three baiocchi of 1799 with the Italian legends L'INCENDI D'RONCIGLIONE and FEDELTA E RELIGIONE, depicting the burning of Ronciglione by the French, was issued at Viterbo.

* Umbria

Julius II (1503–1513), Pius VI (1775–1799).

* Urbino

Julius II (1503–1513), Leo X (1513–1521).
M. M.: URBINO.
Patron and protector: St. Crescentia, martyr, shown S. CRESCENTIANVS. (Feast day April 15.)

Necessity coins were issued at times for the popes; in the sixteenth century after the sack of Rome such coins were struck in the Castle of St. Angelo, and several issues of Pius VI might be termed necessity coins. In addition, there have at times been a few ducal issues such as the Provincia ducats, struck in Champagne for Provence.

There are also extant hundreds of anonymous coins of many of the popes issued at practically all of the mints mentioned, most of which are listed in Cinagli's *Monete dei papi* and to a greater extent in *Corpus nummorum Italicorum.*

Inscriptions

1. A. A. A. F. F.

   Auro Argento Aere Flando Feriundo.   Clement XII

   The *triumviri monetales* were the direc-
   tors of the mint at Rome. They were
   designated III VIR (i.e. Triumvir) AAA
   FF. Flando is from the verb *flo* meaning
   "to pour." *Feriundo* is from the verb
   ferio meaning "to strike." *Auro, argento,*
   and *aere* mean "gold," "silver," and
   "copper." Coins were minted by pour-
   ing or striking; hence the inscription
   means: "By smelting and striking gold,
   silver, or copper," and is shown with
   RESTITVTVM COMMERC.
   (See No. 366.) Plate X, No. 45.

2. ABSIT NISI IN TE GLORIARI   Pius V [1]

   (God) Forbid that one should glory save
   in Thee.   Clement VIII

   "God forbid that I should glory save in
   the cross of our Lord Jesus Christ" (Gal.
   6:14).

3. ABSOLVTO AN IVBILEI   Clement VIII

   "Absolution in the year of jubilee"
   (Lev. 25:11).

4. AB STELLA LVX ORITVR   Alexander VII

   Light from the (eastern) star arises.
   "We have seen His star in the east"
   (Matt. 2:2).

[1] In this case commemorating the victory of the Christian fleet over the Turks
at Lepanto.

5. ABVNDET IN GLORIAM DEI   Clement XII
   May there be abundance to the glory of
   God.
   "Glory to God in the highest and peace
   on earth to men of good will" (Luke
   2:14).

6. ACCENDE LVMEN SENSIBVS   Sede vacante
   Kindle a light for our senses.   1689
   "Tu lux sensibus," etc., from the hymn
   "Aeterne Rerum Conditor."
   As in practically all sede vacante coins,
   the one bearing this inscription shows on
   the obverse the arms of the papal chamberlain, in this case Cardinal Altieri,
   while the reverse design shows a radiant
   dove symbolizing the Holy Ghost.

7. ACCIPE CLAVES REGNI COELORVM   Julius II
   or   Paul II
   ACCIPE CLA RE CELOR.   Alexander VI
   "Receive the keys of the Kingdom of
   Heaven" (Matt. 16:19).
   (See Nos. 50 and 139.)

8. ACCIPIVNT REMISSIONEM   Benedict XIV
   "Let them receive remission" (John
   20:23).
   On a jubilee issue, 1750.

9. A DEO ET PRO DEO   Clement XI
   From God and for the sake of God.

10. AD PATRIAM REDII   Adrian VI
    I have returned to my fatherland.
    Adrian VI, a Dutchman, did much to re-

form patronage practices, held Modena, Parma, and Correggio for the Papal States, and started a crusade against the Turks.

11. ADVENTVS OPTIMI PRINCIPIS   Pius VI
    The coming of the noblest Prince.

12. AERVGO ANIMI CVRA PECVLII   Clement XI
    Care for money is rust of the soul.

13. AETERNA SALVS   Clement VII
    "Eternal salvation" (various passages in the Scriptures).

14. AGIMVS TIBI GRA. OMNIPOTENS DEVS, or   Clement V
    AGIM TIBI GRA   Clement VI
    We give thanks, Almighty God, to Thee.   John XXII

15. AGGREGATO RELIGIO   Gregory XIII
    Religion (has been) increased.   Sixtus V
    "And the churches were confirmed in faith and increased in number daily" (Acts 16:5).

16. ALIIS DIVES   Clement XI
    Rich for others.

17. ALMA ROMA   Plate I, No. 2.   Various popes
    Gracious Rome.

18. ANNO PROPITIATIONIS—Year of propitia-   Various popes
    tion (atonement).   during jubilee
19. ANNO REMISSIONIS—Year of remission.   years.
20. A IVBI; ANN or ANNO IVBELEI—Jubilee year.

21. APERET CLAVS
    Let him open what is closed.
      or
    APERVIT ET CLAVSIT
    He opened it and he closed it.
    Referring to the Porta Sancta or Holy
    Door which is generally depicted on these
    coins as closed, partly open, or entirely
    open.
    (See Nos. 49 and 130.) Plate III, No. 18.

Various jubilee issues

Innocent X
Benedict XIV

22. APERIET DNUS THESAVRVM SVVM
    The Lord will open His treasures.
    "He opened the doors of Heaven and
    rained down manna" (Psalm 76:23–24).

Innocent XII

23. APERIVT CVNCTVS APOSTOLOR. PRINCEPS.
    The Prince of the Apostles opened all
    things.
    On a jubilee issue.
    (See Nos. 21 and 49.)

Pius VI

24. APOSTOLORVM PRINCEPS
    Prince of Apostles.
    This and the preceding inscription refer
    to St. Peter, called the "Prince of Apos-
    tles," which in this case does not mean a
    temporal prince as we know the word but
    rather a leader. Plate XIII, No. 64.

Pius VII

25. AVCTA AD METAVRVM DITION (E)
    Increased by the pleading (of the peo-
    ple) as far as the Metaurus (River).
    The papal territory was increased during

Urban VIII

the pontificate of Urban VIII by the addition of the duchy of Urbino.

26. AVDI DOMINE ET MISERERE
Hear, O Lord, and pity us!
An inscription of supplication or prayer.

Many popes,
notably:
Clement VIII
Pius VI
Pius VII

27. AUXILIUM DE SANCTO
Help from the Sanctuary.
Mittat tibi auxilium de Sancto: "May He
send thee help from the Sanctuary"
(Psalm 19:3). Plate XIV, No. 69.
This inscription was used at various
times from Clement IX (1667–1669) to
sede vacante 1829. The reverse of these
coins nearly always shows a figure representing the Church holding keys and a
tabernacle. One exception is an issue of
Clement IX depicting St. Peter.

Sede vacante
1800–1823 and
1829
Leo XII, Pius
VII,[1] and others

28. AVARVS NON IMPLEBITVR
To the greedy it will not be given.

Innocent XI

29. AVE GRATIA PLENA
"Hail, full of grace" (Luke 1:28).
(See No. 30.)

Gregory XIII

30. AVE MARIA
"Hail, Mary" (from the prayer to the
Blessed Virgin, Luke 1:28).

Paul V

[1] On the edge of the scudo of Pius VII (1815): IN TERRA PAX (Peace on earth).

31. BEARE SOLEO AMICOS MEOS   Gregory XIII
I am accustomed to make my friends   Sixtus V
happy.

32. BEATI PAVPERES   Benedict XIV
Blessed (are the) poor.
"Blessed are ye poor, for yours is the
Kingdom of Heaven" (Luke 6:20); or
"Blessed is he that understandeth the
needy and the poor" (Psalm 40:2).
(See No. 35.)

33. BEATI QVI CVSTODIVNT VIAS MEAS   Sede vacante
Blessed are they who guard my ways.   1555
Quia custodivi vias Domini: "Who guard
the ways of the Lord" (Psalm 17:22).

34. BEATO PIO V   Clement X
To Blessed Pius V.
Clement X beatified Pius V in 1672.
This saint was canonized by Clement XI
in 1712. Pope Pius V was born January
17, 1504, elected pope January 7, 1566,
and died May 1, 1572.

35. BEATVS QVI INTELLIGIT SVPER EGENVM   Innocent XIII
Blessed are they who understand the
poor.
"Blessed is he that understandeth the
needy and the poor" (Psalm 40:2).
(See No. 32.)

36. BELLVM CONTERAM DE TERRA   Innocent XII
I shall destroy war from the earth.
To commemorate the Peace of Ryswick.

37. BENED. NOS OMNI DEVS — Julius II
"May Almighty God bless us" (Psalm 66:8).

38. BENEFAC HUMILI — Benedict XIII
"Aid the lowly" (Matt. 5:3). — Clement XII
Benedict XIV

39. BONONIA DOCET
Bologna teaches.
On coins issued at the Bologna mint—a reference to the famous university established in that city in the thirteenth century. The mint operated from 1191 to 1861. This inscription and the one following first appeared on the bolognino d'oro of the Republic (1376 to 1401) and were used to and including the coinage of Pope Pius VI (1775–1799), after which the Bolognese coinage showed the mint mark "B." Plate II, No. 8.

40. BONONIA MATER STUDIORUM
Bologna, mother of studies.
Shown in various forms, as on coins of Sixtus V, where the obverse shows BONONIA MATER and reverse STUDIORUM. (See Nos. 39 and 41.) Plate I, No. 1.

41. BONONIA PRAECLARA STUDIORUM ALUMNA — Gregory XIII
Bologna, most famous nurse of studies.

42. BON. P. IVL A TYRANNO LIBERAT — Julius II
Pope Julius liberates Bologna from the tyrant.

Referring to the annexation of Emilia, Modena, and Ferrara.

43. CANDOR LUCIS AETERNAE   Clement IX
"The brightness of eternal light" (Wisd. of Sol. 7:26).

44. CAVSA NRAE LAETITIAE   Clement XI
"The cause of our joy" (part of the Litany of the Most Blessed Virgin, or Litany of Loretto).

45. CHARITAS EST DEVS   Gregory XIII
"God is charity" (I John 4:8).

46. CHARITAS FLVIT   Innocent XIII
Charity abounds.
"That your charity may more and more abound" (Phil. 1:9).

47. CIVES SERVATI   Adrian VI
The citizens having been preserved.
A reference to the entering of Parma by papal troops; shown on coins of that mint.

48. CLAVSIS FORIBVS VENIET ET DABIT PACEM   Clement X
When the doors are closed he will come and give peace.
"The doors were shut. . . . Jesus came . . . and said 'Peace be to you'" (John 20:19).
On a jubilee issue.
(See No. 131.) Plate IV, No. 20.

49. CLAVSIT ANNO IVBILEI   Various jubilee
    He closed it in the year of jubilee.   issues

50. CLAVES REGNI COELORUM   Innocent VIII
    "The keys of the Kingdom of Heaven"   Julius II
    (Matt. 16:19).   Leo X
    (See No. 7.)

51. COGENTI INOPIA REI FRVMENTARIAE   Clement VII
    Forced by a lack of grain.
    Issued after the sack of Rome by German
    and Spanish mercenaries under the Holy
    Roman Emperor; with No. 140 on ob-
    verse.

52. COGITO COGITATIONES PACIS   Innocent XII
    I think thoughts of peace" (Jer. 29:11).

53. COLLES FLVENT MEL DE PETRA   Clement X
    The hills pour forth honey from the rock.
    "Filled them with honey out of the rock"
    (Deut. 32:13). Plate III, No. 17.

54. COMMODITAS VIARVM REDVX   Clement XII
    Commodity the restorer of ways (liter-
    ally).
    This inscription has many possible mean-
    ings, several of which are intended, e.g.,
    Trade restores ways of prosperity (allud-
    ing to the coin); Profit restores the
    streets; Civility restores ways of society.
    Plate XII, No. 54.

55. CONCORDIA ALMA ROMA   Julius III
    Concord—gracious Rome.
    Concordat: a treaty of peace or an agree-

ment between the temporal powers and the pope. The inscription in question alludes to the peace between the Farnese family and the state of Parma.

56. (IBI) CONFREGIT POTENTIAS ARCVVM (or AR.) Clement XI
There broke he the powers of the bow.
"There broke he the powers of the bow, the shield, the sword, and all the weapons of war" (Psalm 75:4).
The obverse of coins bearing this inscription show the papal arms; the reverse a bow and arrow pointing upward.

57. CONSERVATÆ PEREVNT Clement XI
Things cared for (on earth) perish.

58. CONTEMPTA PECVNIA DITAT Innocent XIII
Money despised enriches.

59. CORONAT TE IN MISERICORDIA Benedict XIII
He crowns thee in mercy.

60. CRESCENTEM SEQUITUR CURA PECUNIAM Alexander VII
Care follows growing wealth.
The coin shows obverse papal arms; reverse a table with money.

61. CUM EGENIS Innocent XII
"With the needy" (Psalm 69:6).
(See Nos. 118 and 119.)

62. CUM EXULTATIONE Innocent XIII
With exultation.

The coin shows obverse papal arms; reverse two reapers in a field of wheat.

63. CUM ME LAUDARENT SIMUL ASTRA MATU-   Clement X
TINA
When they praise me as the morning star.
"Who is she that cometh forth as the
morning rising, fair as the moon, bright
as the sun?" (Cant. 6:9.)
The Blessed Virgin is often referred to as
Stella Matutina—"Morning Star."

64. CUNCTIS SPRETIS TE SOLAM   Innocent XI
Spurning all things (I worship) Thee
alone.

65. CURABANTUR OMNES   Benedict XIV
All will be cured (or cared for).

66. DABIS DISCERNERE INTER MALVM ET   Clement XII
BONVM
Thou will grant us to discern between
good and evil.
Declina a malo, et fac bonum: "Turn
away from evil and do good" (Psalm 33:
15).
(See No. 234.)

67. DABIT FRVCTVM SVVM IN TEMPORE   Clement X
"He shall give his fruit in due season"
(Psalm 1:3 and Matt. 21:41).

68. DABITVR VOBIS PARACLITVS   Sede vacante
The Holy Spirit will be given you.   1676
"When the Paraclete has come" (John
16:13).

The design symbolizes the Holy Ghost
in the form of a dove, as is usual on sede
vacante coins.

69. DA ET ACCIPE   Clement XI
Give and receive.
"Give and it shall be given to you"
(Luke 6:38).
(See No. 77.)

70. DA NE NOCEAT   Benedict XIII
Give lest evil befall.

71. DA PACEM DOMINE IN DIEBVS NOSTRIS   Clement X
Give peace in our time, O Lord!
"The God of peace shall be with you"
(Phil. 4:9).
(See No. 74.)

72. DA PAUPERI   Innocent XII
Give to the poor.   Clement XIII
"If thou wilt be perfect, go sell what thou
hast and give to the poor" (Matt. 19:21).
(See No. 123.)

73. DAPSILITAS   Paul III
Abundance.
"Whereupon he called it [the city] Abun-
dance" (Gen. 26:33).
The design features a figure representing
Abundance.
This may also refer to a "sacrificial feast"
—an allusion to the Holy Eucharist.

74. DA QUIETA TEMPORA   Sede vacante
Give peaceful times.   1724
(See Nos. 71 and 111.)

75. **DA RECTA SAPERE**   Sede vacante
    May we correctly understand.   1667,1691,1724
    A prayer to the Holy Ghost for guidance
    in the selection of a new pontiff.

76. **DAT ACCIPIT REDDIT**   Gregory XIII
    He gives—he receives—he returns.

77. **DATE ET DABITVR**   Clement XI
    "Give and it will be given" (Luke 6:38).
    Also: "He that giveth to the poor shall
    not want" (Prov. 28:27).
    (See No. 69.)

78. **DAT IN PRETIVM**   Clement XII
    He gives for a reward.

79. **DAT OMNIBVS AFFLVENTER**   Innocent XII
    He gives to all abundantly.
    (See Nos. 82 and 91.)

80. **DECVS PATRIÆ**   Clement XII
    Glory of the Fatherland. Plate XII, No.
    53.

81. **DEDI COREM TE OSTIUM**   Clement X
    I have opened a way before thee.
    A jubilee issue showing the Holy Door.
    "Prepare ye the way of the Lord" (Isa.
    40:3). Plate IV, No. 19.

82. **DEDIT PAVPERIBVS**   Clement XI
    He gave to the poor.
    Dispersit, dedit pauperibus: "He hath
    distributed, he hath given to the poor"
    (Psalm 111:9).
    (See Nos. 79 and 103.)

83. DEDIT PIGNVS   Clement XII
    He gave a pledge.
    In Scripture probably alluding to the
    Lord's pledge to Noah.

84. DEFLUIT ET INFLUIT   Clement XI
    It ebbs and flows. (Literally: It flows
    from above and flows in.) (God's spirit)
    flows from (Him) and inspires (us).
    On the silver scudo of Clement XI, 1717,
    the reverse shows ERID. on a scroll at foot
    of reclining figure, for Eridanus, some-
    times called the Heavenly River, one of
    the southern constellations.

85. DELECTABITVR IN MVLTITVDINE PACIS   Innocent XII
    They (the meek) will rejoice (delight)   Innocent XI
    in abundance of peace.
    "But the meek shall inherit the land and
    shall delight in an abundance of peace"
    (Psalm 36:11).
    Also shown as DELECTABOR   Innocent XI

86. DELICTA OPERIT CHARITAS   Clement XI
    "Charity covers sins" (I Pet. 4:8; also
    Prov. 10:12).

87. DE LVTO FÆCIS   Clement XII
    From the slimy ooze.
    Eduxit me de lacu miseriae, et de luto
    faecis: "He drew me forth from the pit
    of sorrow and the slimy ooze" (Psalm
    39:3).
    (See No. 410.)

88. DE OSCULATÆ SUNT   Clement VIII
    They have kissed.
    Justitia et pax osculatae sunt: "Justice
    and peace have kissed" (Psalm 84:11).
    (See No. 214.)

89. DET DEUS DE COELO   Innocent XII
    May God give from Heaven.
    "I am the living bread which came down
    from Heaven" (John 6:51).

90. DEUS CHARITAS EST   Gregory XIII
    "God is charity" (I John 4:8).
    (See No. 45.)

91. DEUS DAT OMNIBUS AFFLUENTER ET NON   Alexander VII
    IMPROPERAT
    God gives to all abundantly and does not
    delay.
    (See No. 79.)

92. DEVS PACIS CONTERET SATANAM   Innocent XII
    The God of peace will destroy Satan.
    "And the God of peace shall crush Satan
    under your feet speedily" (Rom. 16:20).
    Plate VII, No. 31.

93. DEXTERA DOMINI FECIT VIRTUTEN   Clement XI
    The right hand of the Lord works virtue.

94. DEXTERA TVA DOMINE PERCVSSIT INIM-   Innocent XI
    ICVM [1]
    Thy right hand, O Lord, has struck the
    enemy.

[1] This inscription was first used by Pope St. Pius V on a medal to commemorate the defeat of the Turkish fleet at Lepanto.

*In brachio virtutis tuae dispersisti inimi-
cos tuos:* "With Thy mighty arm Thou
hast scattered Thine enemies" (Psalm
88:11). Plate V, No. 24.

95. DIADEMA SPECIEI DE MANV DOMINI   Clement XII
A diadem of comeliness from the Lord's
hand.

96. DIE NAT. SS MAGNI ET OP (ITER) EP BRU-   Alexander VIII
NONSIS ANACHOR
On the birthday (feast day) of SS Magnus and Bruno, the anchorite, twice of-
fered a bishopric.
A particularly difficult inscription. The
abbreviation OP. makes the exact form
uncertain but the meaning is: "On the
feast day of SS Magnus and Bruno, the
anchorite, twice desired to be a bishop."
St. Bruno was elected bishop of Cologne
but his consecration was prevented by
secular influence. He later refused a
bishopric.
EP: a reference to the bishoprics of these
saints.
ANACHOR: an anchorite, from *anachoreta*
—a hermit; an allusion to the fact that
St. Bruno founded the Carthusian Order
of monks.
St. Magnus died about 750 A.D. St. Bruno,
one of three saints of the name, patron
saint of the Calabrese, founder of the
Carthusian Order of monks, was born in
Cologne in 1030 and died in 1101. He is
usually represented with a death's head

in his hands and a cross. The double
feast day of SS Magnus and Bruno is
September 6.

97. DIGNVS VICTORIAM   Clement XI
Victory to the worthy.

98. DILEXI DECOREM DOMVS TVAE   Clement X
I have loved the beauty of Thy house.   Clement XI
"I have loved, O Lord, the beauty of Thy
house" (Psalm 25:8).
In honor of the Blessed Virgin of Traste-
vere.[1] Plate IX, No. 41.

99. DILIGIT DNVS PORTAS SION   Clement X
The Lord has loved the gates of Sion.
"The Lord loveth the gates of Sion above
all the tabernacles of Jacob" (Psalm
86:2).
Sion was the Holy City of Jerusalem.
This inscription is shown on the reverse
of the jubilee scudo of Clement X, not in
the usual place but on a cornice over the
Holy Door at St. Peter's. Plate IV, No.
21.

100. (AD) DIRIGANTVR PEDES NOSTRI IN VIAM   Paul III
PACIS FOEDERE TVO DEVS
(To) "Direct our feet in the way of peace
and toward God" (Luke 1:79).
(See No. 101.)

101. DIRIGE DNE GRESSVS NROS   Pius II
Lord, direct our steps.

[1] Trastevere is one of the fourteen regions of Rome.

"Direct my steps in Thy paths" (Psalm
16:5).
(See Nos. 100 and 173.)

102. Dispersa Congregat   Gregory XIII
He collects the dispersed (or the wan-
derers).

103. Dispersit Dedit Pavperibvs   Alexander VII
"He distributed, he gave to the poor"   Benedict XIV
(Psalm 111:9).
Reverse design (Alexander VII): St.
Thomas of Villanova helping a poor beg-
ger.
(See No. 82.)   Plate III, No. 14.

104. Dives in Hvmilitate   Innocent XI
Rich in humility.

105. Divinitvs Electo   Julius III
"Elect of God" (Col. 3:12). (Literally:
To one divinely chosen.)
On a jubilee coin the inscription appears
thus: Ivlio III P. M. A. Ivbil Divinitvs
Electo (Julius III, Pontifex Maximus,
jubilee year, Elect of God).
(See No. 364.)

106. Divites in Virtvte   Innocent XI
Rich in virtue.

107. Divitiæ Non Prodervnt   Clement XI
Riches won't help.
"Riches shall not profit in the day of re-
venge" (Prov. 11:4).

108. Divo Thome   Adrian VI
       or   Paul III
    Sanctvs Thomas
    Saint Thomas.
    Used on coins of Parma.

109. Docebit et Svggeret   Sede vacante
    He will teach and bring together.   1691
    "He will teach you all things, and bring
    all things to your mind" (John 14:26).
    (See No. 110.)

110. Docebit Vos Omnia   Sede vacante
    "He will teach you all things" (John   1676
    14:26).   1700
    (See No. 109.)

111. Dona Nobis Pacem   Clement XI
    Grant us peace.
    (See Nos. 71 and 74.) Plate X, No. 46.

112. Ecce Agnvs Dei   Leo X
    Behold the Lamb of God.
    "Behold the Lamb of God, Who takes
    away the sins of the world" (John 1:29).

113. Ecce Fides   Clement VII
    Behold faith.
    On coins of the Parma mint.

114. Ecclesia Romana   Pius II
    The Roman Church.
    (See Nos. 116, 164, and 165.)

115. ECCLESIAE RA. S. RESURE   Leo X
     Holy restoration of the Church at Ra-
     venna.
              also
     ECCLESIAE RAVENNA
     Church of Ravenna.

116. ECCLESIAE RO. FUNDATORES   Julius II
     The founders of the Church at Rome.
     (See Nos. 114, 164, and 165.)

117. EDENT PAVPERES ET SATVRABVNTVR   Benedict XIV
     The poor shall eat and be satisfied.
     Pauperes ejus saturabo panibus (Psalm
     131:15).
     (See No. 128.)

118. EGENO ET PAVPERI   Innocent XII
     For the needy and poor.
     Ego vero egenus, et pauper sum: "But I
     am needy and poor" (Psalm 69:6; Prov.
     31:9; and other passages).
     (See Nos. 61 and 119.) Plate VII, No. 32.

119. EGENO SPES   Innocent XII
     Hope for the needy.
     (See Nos. 61 and 118.)

120. EGO SUM LUX MUNDI   Pius V
     "I am the light of the world" (John   Gregory XIII
     8:12).

121. EGO SUM VIA VERITAS ET VITA   Urban VIII
     "I am the way, the truth and the life"
     (John 14:6).
     (See No. 465.)

122. EGREDIATVR POPVLVS ET COLLIGAT   Innocent XII
Let the people go forth and gather to-
gether.
"Let the people go forth and gather . . ."
(Exod. 16:16).
Obverse: Bust of pope.
Reverse: The people of Israel receiving
manna from Heaven, pictured as a city
in the distance.

123. ELEVAT PAVPERVM   Innocent XII
He helps the poor.
(See No. 72.)

124. EMITTE COELITVS LVCIS TVAE RADIVM   Sede vacante
Send forth a ray of Thy heavenly light.   1740
A prayer to the Holy Ghost for success in
the deliberations leading to the election
of a new pope.

125. EMITTE SPIRITVM TVVM   Sede vacante
Send forth Thy Spirit.   1689
"Send forth Thy spirit, they are created"
(Psalm 103:30).
Referring to the descending of the Holy
Ghost upon the Apostles.

126. ERIGIT ELISOS   Innocent XIII
He raises up those who are cast down.
"The Lord raiseth up all that are cast
down" (Psalm 144:14).
(See No. 427.)

127. ERIT LIGATVM ET IN CAELIS   Innocent XI
"It shall be bound also in Heaven"
(Matt. 16:19).
(See Nos. 132, 223, and 403.)

128. ESURIENTEM NE DESPEXERIS   Clement XI
     Do not despise (or refuse) a hungry man.

129. ESAVRIENTES IMPLEBO   Clement XII
     I will fill (feed) the hungry.
     (See No. 117.)

130. ET CLAVSIT   Jubilee years
     And he closed it.
     Referring to the Porta Sancta or Holy
     Door which is opened in jubilee years,
     every twenty-five years, by the pope with
     many ceremonies.
     (See Nos. 21 and 49.)

131. ET CLAVSO OSTIO ORA PATREM TVVM   Clement X
     "And the door having been closed, be-
     seech thy Father" (John 20:19).
     A jubilee issue.
     (See Nos. 21, 49, and 130.)

132. ET IN COELIS ERIT LIGATVM   Innocent XI
     Will be bound also in Heaven.
     "Whatsoever thou shalt bind upon earth,
     it shall be bound also in Heaven" (Matt.
     16:19).
     (See No. 127.)

133. ET JANVAS COELI APERVIT   Gregory XII
     He opened the doors of Heaven.
     "He opened the doors of Heaven and
     rained down manna" (Psalm 76:23–4).

134. ET MERITAS EXALTATO   Gregory XIII
     And merit is from on High.

Commemorating the Assumption of the
Blessed Virgin Mary.

135. ET MORIENTVR IN SITI   Clement XII
And they will die of thirst.
"They shall not hunger or thirst" (Isa.
49:10).

136. ET PORTAE COELI APERTAE SVNT   Clement VII
And the Gates of Heaven are opened.
"Gate of Heaven" (Gen. 28:17).

137. ET STATUI CUSTODIRE   Sede vacante
And I have placed (him) for a guard.   1591
"Go and set a watchman" (Isa. 21:6).
The reverse design does not show a dove,
as is usual with sede vacante issues. On
this King David is depicted, playing a
harp.

138. ET SUPER HANC PETRAM   Gregory XIII
"And upon this rock" (Matt. 16:18).
(See Nos. 417 and 418.)

139. ET TIBI DABO CLAVES   Gregory XIII
"And to you I will give the keys" (Matt.   Sixtus V
16:19).
(See Nos. 7 and 50.)

140. EX COLLATO ÆRE DE REBVS SACRIS ET   Clement VII
PROPHANIS IN EGENORVM SVBSIDVM.
From treasure gathered from holy and
common things for the help of the needy.
Sacred and profane: At this time any-
thing not pertaining to spiritual things

was called "profane," so the only division
as to art and other objects was between
"sacred" and "profane."
(See No. 51.)

141. Ex Montibvs Pax Orietvr   Alexander VII
And peace will arise on the mountains.
The inscription alludes to the arms of
Alexander VII, which symbolized three
mountain peaks. Hope was thus ex-
pressed that this pontiff would be the
means of bringing peace to Europe.
(See No. 308.)

142. Exvrgat D et Dissipentvr Inimici Ejvs   Pius II
Grant that God may arise and scatter His
enemies.
"Let God arise, and let His enemies be
scattered; and let them that hate Him flee
from before His face" (Psalm 67:2).
(See No. 143.)

143. Exvrgat Devs   Pius IV
"May God arise" (Psalm 67:2).
(See No. 142.)

144. F. or Fecit
Originally *Me fecit:* "He engraved it."
After the names or signatures of engrav-
ers, such as "Hameranus F.," etc.

145. Faciant Ivstitias (et) Eleemosyn   Clement XI
Let them do justice and give alms.
"Neglect not to pray, and to give alms"
(Ecclus. 7:10, and elsewhere in the Scrip-
tures).

146. (ET) FACTVS EST IN PACE LOCVS EJVS   Innocent XII
His place is made in peace.
"His place is made in peace and in Sion
his dwelling" (Psalm 75:3). Plate VII,
No. 34.

147. FAC VT IVVET   Innocent XII
Do as is pleasing.

148. FEDELTA E RELIGIONE   Sede vacante
Honesty and religion.   1799
Obverse: Inscription as above and head
of the Blessed Virgin.
Reverse: L'INCENDIO DI RONCIGLIONE
ANNO 1799, with view of burning city.
(See No. 224.)

149. FER AVXILIVM   Clement X
Give aid.

150. FERRO NOCENTIVS AVRVM   Innocent XII
Gold is more harmful than steel (iron).

151. FIAT PAX   Clement XI
Let there be peace.
"Peace upon Israel" (Psalm 127:6).
(See Nos. 152 and 153.)

152. FIAT PAX IN VIRTUTE TUA   Clement VII,
"Let there be peace in thy strength"   Paul III, Inno-
(Psalm 121:7). Plate VII, No. 33.   cent XII, Clement XI, Clem-
ent XIV

153. FIAT PAX SUPER ISRAEL   Clement XI
"Let there be peace over Israel" (Psalm
127:6).
(See No. 151.)

154. FIDEM SERVAVI   Sede vacante
     I have preserved the faith.   1590

155. FIXA MANEBIT   Clement XI
     She will remain set (or fixed).
     Obverse: Papal arms.
     Reverse: An anchor standing upright on
     the waves; a symbol of faith.

156. FLORET IN DOMO DOMINI   Pius VI
     Flourish (prosper) in the House of the
     Lord.
     Beati, qui habitant in domo tua Domini:
     "Blessed are they that dwell in the House
     of the Lord" (Psalm 83:5).

157. FOEDVS EST INTER ME ET TE   Clement XII
     "There is a covenant between me and
     thee" (Gen. 17:7, and elsewhere).

158. FOENERATVR DOMINO QVI MISERETVR   Clement XI
     PAVPERI (or PAVPERIS)
     He lends to God who aids the poor.
     "He that hath mercy on the poor, lend-
     eth to the Lord; and He will repay him"
     (Prov. 19:17).   Benedict XIII

159. FOENVS PECVNIÆ FVNVS EST ANIMÆ   Clement XI
     Interest on money is smoke of the soul.

160. FONTIS ET FORI ORNAMEN   Clement XI
     An ornament to the spring and the forum.
     This is the literal translation. The design
     explains the inscription, consisting of the
     fountain and obelisk and a prospect of

the Plaza della Rotonda as a reverse of
one variety of scudo, while a second variety shows simply the fountain and obelisk. The obverse of each shows the papal
arms. The inscription on the second variety is as above, except that the last word
is spelled *ornamento*.

The Plaza della Rotonda, formerly the
Plaza della Pantheon, was the site of the
Pantheon, a great temple of Jupiter,
built by Agrippa in ancient times and
dedicated to all the gods of paganism. It
is now the site of the Temple of S. Maria
Rotonda, dedicated by Pope Boniface IV
to Our Lady of Martyrs in the year 608,
when thirty-eight cartloads of martyrs'
relics were brought there. A remarkable
fact about the church is that it has no
windows; ventilation and light are secured through a hole in the roof. Plate
XI, No. 49.

161. Fore Tvtvm Praesidivm   Sixtus V
To be hereafter a safe defense.

162. Frustra Vigilat Qui Custodit   Clement XII
He watcheth in vain that keepeth it.
Nisi Dominus custodient cititatem, frus-
tra vigilat qui custodit eam: "Unless the
Lord keep the city, he watcheth in vain
that keepeth it" (Psalm 126:1). Plate XI,
No. 51.

163. Funda Nos in Pace   Innocent XI
Establish us in peace.
From the hymn *"Ave Maris Stella."*

164. FUNDATORES ROMAN ECCLESIAE   Leo X
 Founders of the Roman Church.
 (See Nos. 114, 116, and 165.)

165. FUNDATORI ECCLESIAE   Julius II
 To the founder of the Church.
 (See Nos. 114, 116, and 164.)

166. GENS ET REGNUM QUOD NON SERVIERIT   Julius III
 TIBI PERIBIT
 The people and the nation which will
 not serve Thee will perish.
 "Nations and kings shall do service to
 Him—Yea, all the kings of the earth shall
 worship Him; all nations shall do Him
 service" (Psalm 71:11).

167. GENVS ALTO A SANGUINE   Clement XII
 Sprung from high (noble) blood.
 Obverse: Papal arms.
 Reverse: St. Andrew Corsini accepting a
 miter from an angel.
 Clement XII, whose family name was
 Lorenzo Corsini, was of the same family
 as St. Andrew Corsini.

168. GLORIA IN EXCELSIS DEO   Innocent VIII
 Glory to God in the highest.
 "Glory to God in the highest, and peace
 on earth to men of good will" (Luke
 2:14).

169. GLORIOSI PRINCIPES   Clement VIII
 Glorious princes.
 (See No. 170.)

170. GLORIOSI PRINCIPES TERRAE   Pius V
Glorious princes of earth.
"Prince of the Kings of the earth" (Rev.
1:5).
(See No. 169.)

171. GRATIA VOBIS ET PAX MULTIPLICETUR   Innocent XII
Grace and peace to you abundantly.
(Literally: Grace and peace be multi-
plied unto you.) Plate VIII, No. 36.

172. GRATIE DEI OMNE BONUM   Innocent XII
"Thank God for all good" (Col. 1:3, and
frequent elsewhere in the Scriptures).

173. GRESSUS MEOS DIRIGE   Innocent XI
Direct my steps.
"Direct my steps in thy paths" (Psalm
16:5).
(See No. 100.)

174. HABETIS PAVPERIS   Clement XII
You have the poor.
"For the poor you have always with you"
(Matt. 26:11).

175. HAEC AVTEM QVÆ PARASTI CVIVS ERVNT   Alexander VII
Whose will these things be that you have
prepared?

176. HAEC PORTA DOMINI   Clement VIII
This is the door of the Lord.   Clement X
A jubilee inscription.
(See No. 322.)

177. HAEC QVÆ ATTVLIT SALVTEM　　　Paul III
This which bears salvation.
(See No. 186.)

178. HILAREM DATOREM DILIGIT DEVS　　　Alexander VII
"The Lord loveth a cheerful giver" (II
Cor. 9:7).
(See No. 272.)

179. HINC FIDES ET FORTITVDO　　　Sixtus V
Hence faith and fortitude.
"Grace and fortitude" (Acts 6:8).

180. HODIE SALVS FACTA EST MVNDO　　　Leo X
Today salvation has come to the world.
"This day is salvation come to this
house" (Luke 19:9).

181. (HOMINIBVS VOLVNTATIS) QVI DILIGVNT　　Urban VIII
NOMEN TVVM
(For men of good will) who love Thy
name.
(See No. 168.)

182. I. E. M. I. S. S.　　　Alexander VII
Ivstitia Eivs Manet in Secvla Secvlorvm
May His justice remain forever and ever.
"Glory and wealth shall be in His house
and His justice endureth forever and
ever" (Psalm 111:3).

183. I ⧓ S COR.　　　Gregory XIII
Sacred Heart of Jesus.[1]
Issued in 1582 to commemorate the
founding of the Jesuit College at Rome.

[1] IHS also stands for *Jesus Hominem Salvator:* Jesus, Saviour of Man.

184. ILLUMINET CORDA NOSTRA   Sede vacante
May He illuminate our hearts.   1740
A prayer to the Holy Ghost for guidance
in selecting a new pontiff.

185. ILLUXIT ILLUCESCAT ADHUC   Sede vacante
He has given light—may He continue to   1669
give light.
(*Cf.* Eph. 5:8–11.)
A prayer to the Holy Ghost. Plate III,
No. 15.

186. IMAGO SALVTIS   Gregory XIII
The image of salvation.
Depicting Veronica's veil.
(See No. 177.)

187. IMPERAT AVT SERVIT   Clement XI
He commands or serves.
"Commands and teaches" (I Tim. 4:11).

188. IMPLETI ILLUSIONIBUS   Clement XII
Filled with illusions.
Lumbi mei impleti sunt illusionibus:
"My loins are filled with illusions"
(Psalm 37:8).

189. IN CHARITATE MULTIPLICABITUR   Benedict XIII
He will be increased (grow strong) by
charity.
"And may the Lord multiply you, and
make you abound in charity towards one
another" (I Thess. 3:12).

190. IN CIBOS PAVPERVM   Clement XII
Feed the poor.
One of the corporal works of mercy.

191. In Egenos   Innocent XIII
     For the poor.
     (See No. 61.)

192. Infunde Amorem Cordibus   Sede vacante
     Pour love into (our) hearts.   1655
     "The charity of God is poured abroad in   1939
     our hearts by the Holy Ghost who is
     given to us" (Rom. 5:5).
     An example of the unchanging prayer
     to the Holy Ghost. The same inscription
     was used after an interval of almost three
     hundred years, and the designs follow
     the same general plan.
     On the scudo of 1655, obverse: Arms
     with canopy of the papal camerlingo, or
     chamberlain, Cardinal Barberini. Re-
     verse: A dove.
     On the ten and five lire silver, 1939,
     obverse: Arms of the papal chamberlain,
     Cardinal Pacelli. Reverse: A radiant
     dove.

193. In Hoc Signo Vinces   Julius II
     By this sign thou shalt conquer.
     This inscription dates back to Constan-
     tine the Great, who used it on his coins,
     since he ascribed his great victories to a
     sign of the cross in the sky, surrounded by
     these words. It has been used at times on
     coins of other Catholic countries, notably
     on the gold cruzados of Portugal.

194. In Honorem S. Theodori Mar.   Clement XI
     In honor of St. Theodore the martyr.

St. Theodore lived in the third century
and suffered martyrdom by burning at
the stake in 306. A very old church, the
Church of St. Theodore di Palatine in
Rome, is visited by the poor, who bring
their children there for aid in sickness.
The same inscription and design has
been used on a medal. Plate X, No. 44.

195. In Ipso Edocti Estis   Sede vacante
     You will be learned in Him.   1730

196. In Nomine Domini   Paul III
     In the name of God.

197. In Omnem Terram Exivit Sonus   Julius II
     Corum
     The sound of their songs has gone forth
     into all the earth.
     "Their sound hath gone forth into all the
     earth; and their words unto the ends of
     the world" (Psalm 18:5).

198. Inopiæ Sit Supplementum   Clement XI
     Let there be plenty for the needy.

199. In Petra Exaltasti Me   Clement VIII
     "On a rock thou hast safely set me"   Sede vacante
     (Psalm 60:3).   1605

200. In Portas Opera Ejus   Clement X
     His works are at the gates (are evident).
     "Behold, I stand at the gate" (Rev.
     3:30).

201. In Sudore Vultis Tui   Clement XI
    In the sweat of thy face.
    "In the sweat of thy face thou shalt eat
    thy bread" (Gen. 3:19).

202. In Te Domine Speravi   Pius V
    "In Thee, O Lord, have I hoped" (Psalm
    30:2).

203. In Te Signum Nostrae Redemptionis   Sixtus V
    In Thee is the sign of our redemption.

204. In Te Sitio   Sixtus V
    For Thee do I thirst.
    "My soul hath thirsted after the strong
    living God" (Psalm 41:3).
    Obverse: Bust of Pope left.
    Reverse: Kneeling figure of St. Francis
    receiving the stigmata from Heaven.

205. In Testimonia Tui et Non in Avari-   Clement XI
    TIAM
    In testimony to Thee, and not in avarice.
    "Incline my heart in testimony to Thee,
    and not in avarice" (Psalm 118:36).

206. In Verbo Tuo   Innocent X
    In Thy word.
    Frequent in the Scriptures.

207. In Via Virtvtis   Clement XII
    In the way of virtue.
    Frequent in the Scriptures.

208. Ipse Est Pax Nostra   Innocent XII
    He Himself is our peace.

Obverse: Papal arms.
Reverse: The Saviour—globe in one
hand.

209. Isti Sunt Patres Tui Verique Pastores   Pius VIII
These are thy fathers and thy true
pastors.
"I will set up pastors over them and they
shall feed them" (Jer. 23:4).
Obverse: Bust of Pope right.
Reverse: Standing figures SS Peter and
Paul.
(See No. 311.)   Plate XV, No. 73.

210. Iter Para Tutum   Sixtus V
"Prepare a safe way" (Isa. 40:3).   Urban VII
                                                Sede vacante
                                                    1590
                                                Gregory XIV
                                                Gregory XV

211. Iuncta Operibus   Gregory XIII
Joined in works.
(Cf. Rom. 4.)

212. Iusti Intrabunt in Eam   Clement VII
The just will enter into it.   and others
"Open ye the gates, and let the just na-
tion, that keepeth the truth, enter in"
(Isa. 26:2).
Also shown as Ivsti Intra Rvnt in Eam
on jubilee triple julio, 1525.

213. Ivstis Patet   Gregory XIII
It is open to the just.
A jubilee issue.

214. IVSTITIAE PACISQUE CVLT   Alexander VI
Worshiper of justice and peace.
Of the same source as No. 88.
Also IVSTIT PACIS Q CVLT—AN IVBILE
MD on jubilee testone of Alexander VI—
the first dated jubilee coin, 1500.

215. IVSTITIA RESVRGENS   Gregory XIII
Justice rising again.
On a rare double julio of Gregory XIII,
1575.

216. IUVAT ET NOCET   Benedict XIII
He aids and harms.
(See No. 427.)

217. LABOR ADDITUS   Clement XII
Added labor.
". . . and he that addeth knowledge,
addeth also labor" (Eccles. 1:18).

218. LAETIFICAT CIVITATEM   Clement XI
He makes the people rejoice.
"There was therefore great joy in that
city" (Acts 8:9).
The initials Io. Ho. on the half scudo of
Clement XI stand for John (Ioannes)
Hortolani, or Ortolani, the engraver.

219. LEGIONE AD BELLUM SACRUM INSTRUCTA   Alexander VIII
When a legion had been marshaled for
the holy war.
Referring to the wars of Christian nations against the Turks. Plate VI, No. 28.

220. LETAMINI GENTES   Gregory XIII
     Rejoice, ye nations.
     "The city rejoiceth" (Prov. 11:10).

221. LEVATA ONERE PATRIA   Gregory XIII
     The fatherland was raised by his labor.
     Great public works were accomplished
     during Gregory's pontificate, including
     the founding of English, German, Greek,
     and other colleges in Rome.

222. LIBERTAS ECCLESIASTICUS   Paul III
     The freedom of the Church.

223. LIGAT ET SOLVIT   Sixtus V
     He binds and looses.
     "And I will give to thee the keys of the
     Kingdom of Heaven and whatsoever thou
     shalt bind upon earth, it shall be bound
     also in Heaven, and whatsoever you shall
     loose upon earth, shall be loosed also in
     Heaven" (Matt. 16:19).
     (See No. 403.)

224. L'INCENDIO DI RONCIGLIONE   Sede vacante
     The fire of Ronciglione.   1799
     (See No. 148.)

225. LOQUETUR PACEM GENTIBUS   Innocent XII
     He (God) will speak peace to the na-
     tions.
     (See No. 294.)

226. LUMEN AD REVELATIONEM GENTIUM   Gregory XVI
     "A light for the revelation of the gen-
     tiles" (Luke 2:32).

Obverse: Bust of Pope left.
Reverse: Presentation of the child Jesus
in the Temple. Plate XV, No. 75.

227. LUMEN RECTIS   Clement XII
Light to the righteous.
Lux orta justo, et rectis, corde laetitia:
"Light is risen to the just, and gladness
to such as are right of heart" (Psalm
96:11).

228. LUMEN SEMITIS MEIS   Sede vacante
Light for my paths.   1730

229. LUMINARIA VERAE FIDEI   Julius II
Lamps of true faith.
"Lamp" appears many times in the Old
and New Testaments, generally as a sign
of faith.

230. LUX MUNDI   Pius V
"Light of the world" (John 8:12).

231. LUX VERA IN TENEBRIS LUCET   Leo X
The true light will shine in the darkness.
". . . that we may declare His virtues,
Who has called us out of darkness to His
admirable light" (I Peter 2:9).

232. MACULA NON EST IN TE   Benedict XIV
There is not a spot in thee.
"Thou art all fair, my love, and there is
not a spot in thee" (Cant. 4:7).
(See No. 429.)

233. MAGNARVM ALARVM   Innocent XIII
    (Beneath the shadow) of mighty wings.
    Obverse: Bust of Pope right.
    Reverse: An eagle.
    The eagle pictured on reverse of coins
    bearing this motto was part of the armo-
    rial bearings of the house of Este. Com-
    pare coins of the rulers of Este, Modena,
    and Ferrara showing the motto SUB UM-
    BRA ALARUM TUARUM (Under the
    shadow of Thy wings).[1]

234. MALUM MINUIT BONUM AUGET   Clement X
    Evil has diminished—good is increasing.
    "Turn away from evil and do good"
    (Psalm 33:15).
    Scudo AR.
    Obverse: Bust of Pope right.
    Reverse: Figures representing Clemency
    and Liberality.
    (See No. 66.)

235. MANVM TVAM APERVIT INOPE   Clement XI
    He opened his hand to the needy.
    "She hath opened her hand to the needy,
    and stretched out her hands to the poor"
    (Prov. 31:20).
    (See No. 306.)

236. MELIORA MANENT   Julius III
    Let better things remain.

[1] See coins of Emilia, Correggio, Modena, and Ferrara, *Corpus nummorum Itali-corum*, Vol. IX.

237. MELIUS EST DARE QUAM ACCIPERE   Innocent XI
"It is better to give than receive" (Ec-
clus. 4:36).
Several varieties with inscription in
scroll, wreath, shield, or square.

238. MENTES TUORUM VISITA   Sede vacante
Visit the minds of Thy (faithful).   1676
A prayer to the Holy Ghost.

239. ME SEQUERE   Gregory XIII
"Follow me" (Matt. 9:9 and 20:21).
(See No. 392.)

240. MISERICORS ET JVSTVS   Clement XIII
Merciful and just.
"He that followeth justice and mercy,
shall find life, justice and glory" (Prov.
21:21).

241. MISIT D. ANG. SVVM ET LIBERAVIT ME   Clement VII
The Lord has sent His angel and deliv-
ered me.
"The Lord hath sent His Angel and hath
delivered me out of the hand of Herod"
(Acts 12:11).
(See No. 242.)

242. MISIT DOMINVS ANGELVM SVVM   Sede vacante
also   1590
MISIT DOMIN. ANGE. SVVM   Gregory XIV
The Lord has sent His Angel.
(See No. 241.)

243. MODICE FIDEI QVARE DVBITATIS D (OMI-   Paul II
     NVS) ADJVVA NOS
     "Why do ye doubt, O ye of little faith—
     O Lord help us" (John 20:26–31) .
     MODICE FIDEI QVARE DVBITATIS   Calixtus III
     MODICE FIDEI QVARE DUBITASTI   Sixtus IV

244. MODICVM JVSTO   Innocent XI
     "A little to the just man" (Psalm 36:16) .   Clement XI
                                              Benedict XIV

245. MONE NOVA   Sixtus V
     New coinage.
     Sixtus V did much to eliminate billon
     coinage and to introduce the use of pure
     silver, especially in the dollar-size coin
     later called the scudo.

246. MONSTRA TE ESSE MATR. or MATREM   Urban VIII
     Show thyself a mother.
     From the hymn *"Ave Maris Stella."*
     Obverse: Papal arms.
     Reverse: The Blessed Virgin and Child.

247. MORTIFERA NON NOCEBVNT   Paul V
     Deadly things will do no harm.
     ". . . if they drink any deadly thing, it
     shall not hurt them" (Mark 16:18) .
     Commemorating the miracle of St. Paul's
     conversion. (*Cf.* Acts 9.)

248. MULTOS PERDIDIT AURUM   Innocent XI
     Gold has destroyed many.
     MULTOS PERDIDIT ARGENTUM   Clement XI
     Silver has destroyed many.

"For gold and silver hath destroyed
many" (Ecclus. 8:3).

249. MUNDI REVERTVNTVR   Pius VI
Worlds will return.
A jubilee inscription probably meaning,
"Worlds will return to grace."

250. NAVIS AETERNAE SALUTIS   Julius II
Ship of eternal salvation.   Leo X
A reference to the Catholic Church.

251. NEC CITRA NEC ULTRA   Alexander VII
Neither too near nor too far.
Obverse: Papal arms.
Reverse: A hand holding a scale.

252. NE FORTE OFFENDICULUM FIAT   Clement XII
Lest perchance there be some small cause
of offence.
*Ne forte offendos ad lapidem pedum
tuum:* "Lest perchance, thou dash thy
foot against a stone" (Psalm 90:12).

253. NE OBLIVISCARIS PAUPERUM   Innocent XII
Forget not the poor.   Clement XI
Non est oblitus clamorem pauperum:
"He hath not forgotten the cry of the
poor" (Psalm 9:13).

254. NE PROIICIAS ME IN TEMPORE SENEC-   Clement X
    TUTIS
"Desert me not in the time of old age"
(Psalm 91:11).
Obverse: Papal arms.
Reverse: David playing on harp.

255. NEQUE DIVITIAS   Clement XI
   Nor riches.   Innocent XI
   "Riches will not profit in the day of re-
   venge" (Prov. 11:4).
   (See Nos. 107 and 275.)

256. NESCIT TARDA MOLIMINA   Sede vacante
   He does not endure slow enterprises.   1724

257. NIGRA SED FORMOSA   Gregory XIII
   (I am) Black but beautiful.
   "I am black but beautiful, O ye daugh-
   ters of Jerusalem, as the tents of cedar,
   as the curtains of Solomon" (Cant. 1:4).
   Alluding to the Church reviled and
   called black by its enemies, but really
   beautiful and fair.

258. NIHIL AVARO SCELESTIVS   Innocent XI
   There is nothing more criminal than a
   greedy man.

259. NOCET MINUS   Clement XI
   It harms less. Plate V, No. 25.

260. NOLI AMARE NE PERDAS   Innocent XII
   Do not love (money) lest you be lost.
   (See No. 262.)

261. NOLI ANXIUS ESSE   Innocent XI
   Do not be anxious.
   "Be not anxious for goods unjustly got-
   ten" (Ecclus. 5:10).

262. NOLI COR APPONERE   Clement XI
     Do not set your heart upon (riches).
     NOLITE COR APPONERE   Innocent XI
     "If wealth flow in, set not your heart
     thereon" (Psalm 61:11).
     (See Nos. 263, 269, and 394.)

263. NOLI LABORARE UT DITERIS   Clement XI
     Do not labor to be rich.
     "Labor not to be rich" (Prov. 23:4).
     (See Nos. 262, 269, and 394.)

264. NOLI ME TANGERE   Gregory XIII
     Touch me not.   Sixtus V
     Nolite tangere christus meos: "Touch   Sede vacante
     not My anointed ones" (Psalm 104:15;   1590
     also various places in the New Testa-
     ment).
     The reverse design in each case shows a
     figure of Mary Magdalen. See John
     20:17: "Jesus saith to her: Do not touch
     me, for I am not yet ascended to my
     Father."
     Shown once in error NUUN MEI ANGERE   Gregory XIII

265. NOLITE THESAURIZARE   Innocent XI
     Do not lay in treasure.
     "Do not store up wealth" (Ecclus. 31:8).
     (See No. 263.)

266. NON ALIUNDE SALUS   Paul III
     Salvation is in no other.
     "Neither is there salvation in any other"
     (Acts 4:12).

267. Non Apparentium est Fides   Gregory XIII
     Faith has no price.
     "Or what shall a man give in exchange
     for his soul?" (Mark 8:37.)

268. Non Aurum sed Nomen   Clement XI
     Not in gold but (His) name.
     (See No. 273.)

269. Non Concupisces Argentum   Clement XI
     Do not seek (desire) wealth.
     "Labor not to be rich" (Prov. 23:4).
     (See Nos. 262 and 263.)

270. Non Deficiet Fides   Gregory XIII
     Let not faith decrease. (No lessening of
     faith.)
     (See Nos. 283 and 284.)

271. Non Est Pax   Clement XII
     There is no peace.

272. Non ex Tristitia Avt ex Necessitate   Alexander VII
     Not with sadness or of necessity.
     "Everyone as he hath determined in his
     heart, not with sadness or of necessity:
     for God loveth a cheerful giver" (II Cor.
     9:7).
     (See No. 178.)

273. (Et) Non in Avaritiam   Clement XI
     Not in avarice.
     "Incline my heart unto Thy command-
     ments, and not unto avarice" (Psalm
     118:36).
     (See Nos. 205 and 268.)

274. Non Praevalebunt   Clement VIII
    Shall not prevail.
    "The gates of Hell shall not prevail"
    (Matt. 16:18).
    (See No. 323.)

275. Non Proderunt in Die Ultionis   Innocent XI
    They will be of no avail on the day of
    vengeance (judgment).
    "Riches shall not profit in the day of re-
    venge" (Prov. 11:4).
    (See No. 255.) Plate VI, No. 26.

276. Non Relinquam Vos Orphanos   Sede vacante
    "I will not leave you orphans, I will come   1846
    to you" (John 14:18).
    Obverse: Arms of Papal Camerlingo Car-
    dinal Riario Sforza.
    Reverse: The Holy Ghost symbolized by
    a dove.
    (See No. 279.)

277. Non Sibi sed Aliis   Innocent XII
    Not for Himself but for others.
    A reference to the Holy Eucharist.
    Obverse: Papal arms.
    Reverse: A pelican feeding her young
    with her own blood, a symbol of the
    Holy Eucharist.

278. Non Sit Tecum in Perditionem   Innocent XII
    May it (money) not be with you for de-
    struction.

279. Non Vos Relinquam Orphanos   Sede vacante
    I will not leave you orphans.   1700
    "I will not leave you orphans, I will come   1721
    to you" (John 14:18).   1724
    (See No. 276.)

280. Nostra Redemptio   Julius II
    Our redemption.

281. Novit Jvstvs Cavsam Pavpervm   Innocent XII
    The just do not forget the cause of the   Benedict XIV
    poor.
    "The just taketh notice of the cause of
    the poor" (Prov. 29:7).

282. Nullus Argento Color. Est Avaris   Innocent XIII
    There is no color to silver for the greedy.
    The meaning of this is that the rich sub-
    jects of the pope should be generous in
    their charities.

283. Nunquam Deficiet   Gregory XIII
    He will never fail.   Sixtus V
    (See Nos. 270 and 284.)

284. Nunquam Sitiet   Gregory XIII
    He will never thirst.
    "He that believeth in Me will never
    thirst" (John 6:35).
    This inscription is quite similar to the
    one immediately preceding. The latter,
    No. 283, is another form of No. 270, Non
    deficiet fides (No lessening of faith).

285. NUNTIA PACIS   Innocent XII
     Announce peace.

286. NUTANTIA CORDA TU DIRIGAS   Sede vacante
     Direct our wavering hearts.   1740
     "And the Lord direct your hearts"
     (II Thess. 3:5).

287. OB SANCTIFICATIONEM IVBILEI   Clement X
     For sanctification of Jubilee.
     "Because of the sanctification of the
     Jubilee" (Lev. 25:12).

288. OBLECTAT JUSTOS MISERICORDIA   Clement XIII
     He delights the just by His mercy.

289. OCULI EJUS IN PAUPEREM   Benedict XIV
     His (God's) eyes look upon the poor
     man.
     Oculi ejus in pauperem respiciunt; pal-
     pebrae ejus interrogant filios hominum:
     "God's eyes look upon the poor man;
     His eyelids examine the sons of men"
     (Psalm 10:5).

290. OMNIA TVTA VIDES ROMA   Julius III
     Thou seest all things safe in Rome.
     Alluding to the establishment of peace
     between Parma and Tuscany.

291. OPVS JVSTITIAE PAX   Innocent XII
     The work (fruit) of justice is peace.   Sede vacante
     "The work of justice shall be peace"   1939
     (Isa. 32:17).

On the half scudo of Innocent XII, obverse: Pope's bust right.

Reverse: A figure representing Peace standing.

On the silver five and ten lire sede vacante 1939 Opvs Ivstitiae Pax is included in the arms of the Papal Chamberlain Cardinal Pacelli, now Pope Pius XII.

292. Oratione et Ieivnio—Deo Exercitvvm   Clement XI
By fasting and prayer—to the God of armies.

Obverse: Pope's bust right.

Reverse: Oratione et Ieivnio, and two figures preparing a sacrificial altar on which is inscribed Deo Exercitvvm.

293. Ostivm Coeli Apertvm In Terris
The mouth of Heaven is open to the earth.

A jubilee inscription.

294. Pacem Loquetur Gentibus   Innocent XII
He speaks peace to the nations.
(See No. 225.) Plate VIII, No. 35.

295. Pacem Meam Do Vobis   Leo X
I give you my peace.   Clement X
Issued on the establishment of peace between the old families of Orsini and Colonna.

296. Paci Pontificiæ S. P. Q. B.   Paul III
For the pontifical peace—the Senate and the people of Bologna.

297. PARACLITUS ILLUMINET   Sede vacante
     May the Paraclete (Holy Ghost) en-   1700
     lighten.
     "When the Paraclete has come" (John
     16:13).

298. PARATE VIAM DOMINI   Innocent XII
     "Prepare the way of the Lord" (Isa.
     40:3).
     Reverse: John the Baptist.

299. PASTOR DOCTOR   Julius II
     Shepherd—Teacher (freely).   Leo X
     "He gave some, apostles . . . and some,
     pastors and doctors" (Eph. 4:11).

300. PASTORI ET PRINCIPI SENATUS BONON-   Benedict XIV
     IENSIS
     To the Pastor and Prince—the Bologna
     Senate. Benedict XIV (Prospero Lamb-
     ertini) was archbishop of Bologna prior
     to his election as pope.

301. PASTORIOVIVM VAS ELECTI   Gregory XIII
              or   Sede vacante
     PASTOR OVI VAS ELEC.   1535
     Vessel of election of pastors.   Sixtus V
     "And the Lord said to him: Go thy way;
     for this man [Paul] is to me a vessel of
     election. . . ." (Acts 9:15).
     (See No. 457.)

302. PATER QUI MISIT ME TRAHET EVM   Sede vacante
     The Father who sent me will draw him.   1700
     "No man can come to me, except the

Father, who hath sent me, draw him; and I will raise him up in the last day" (John 6:44).
Obverse: Arms of Papal Chamberlain Cardinal Spinola.
Reverse: The Holy Ghost in the form of a dove.

303. Patrie et Scientarivm Institvto Magnifice Avcto SPQB   Benedict XIV
The Senate and the people of Bologna (honor him) for an improved fatherland and enlarged Institute of Science.
Pope Benedict XIV was renowned for his many scientific studies and for his help in enlarging the Vatican Library, opening the Museum of Sciences, and many other notable achievements in the field of education and science.

304. Patrim S. Petri   Benedict XI
Patrimony of St. Peter.[1]   Benedict XII
Also shown Patr. Bea. Pe.   John XXII

305. Patri Patriae   Benedict XIV
For the father of his country.
(See No. 327.)

306. Pauperi Porrige Manum Tuam   Clement XI
Stretch forth thy hand over the poor.   Clement XII
"Stretch forth thy hand to the poor that   Benedict XIV
thy expiation and thy blessing may be   Pius VII
perfected" (Ecclus. 7:36).
(See Nos. 235 and 337.) Plate XIV, No. 67.

---

[1] Patrimony of St. Peter: Part of the Papal States, in Tuscany.

307. PAX DEI CUSTODIAT CORDA VESTRA   Clement X
May the peace of the Lord guard your
hearts.
"Let the peace of Christ rejoice in your
hearts" (Col. 3:15).

308. PAX ORIETVR EX MONTIBVS   Alexander VII
Peace will come over the mountains.
(See No. 141.)

309. PAX ROMANA   Julius II
Peace of Rome.
On double julio of Julius II commemorating the reconciliation of the families
of Orsini and Colonna.[1]

310. P. C. I. R. C.   Pius XI
Pax Christi in Regno Christi.
The peace of Christ in the Kingdom of
Christ.
"Christ the King" (Luke 23:2).
These letters appear on the ten lire silver
of Pius XI, 1936, on the edge.

311. PE (TRUS) AP (OSTO) LVS PAV (LVS) DOC-   Various popes
(TOR) GENTIVM
Peter the Apostle and Paul, Doctor of the
Gentiles.

[1] Orsini and Colonna: Old Roman families who trace their origin as far back
as the old Roman Empire. Their names are represented in their coats of arms:
Orsini, from *orso*, a bear; Colonna, column. Members of these families, which
were powerful in church and state affairs for centuries, attained papal honor:
Odo Colonna (Pope Martin V, 1417–1431) and Peter Francis Orsini (Pope Benedict XIII, 1724–1730), the latter long after the Orsini had ceased to be influential.
    The coat of arms of the Colonna family is shown on some coins of Martin V,
while both Colonna and Orsini are represented in the arms on coins of the Senate
of Rome, as early as 1292.

"I am appointed a preacher and an apostle, a doctor of the Gentiles, in faith and truth" (I Timothy 2:7).
(See No. 209.)

312. PECCATA ELEEMOSYNIS REDIME   Innocent XII
Redeem (atone, pay for) your sins by almsgiving. Plate IX, No. 38.
PECCATA REDIME   Innocent XII
"Your sins are redeemed" (John 20:23).

313. PETENTI TRIBVE   Benedict XIII
Give to him that asks.
"Ask and it shall be given to you" (Matt. 7:7).

314. PETRE ECCE TEMPLUM TUUM   Leo X
Peter, behold your temple.

315. PETRE PASCE OVES MEAS   Sixtus IV
"Peter, feed My sheep" (John 21:17).

316. PIETATIS VITAEQUE   Gregory XIII
Of piety and life.
On a jubilee issue.

317. PLACIDO SAPORE DORMIEBAT   Clement XI
He slept peacefully and quietly.

318. PONS CIVITA CASTELLANAE   Clement XI
The Bridge of Castellana (the turreted state).
Obverse: Papal arms.
Reverse: Prospect of the bridge and city in distance. This inscription is shown in

the exergue, the main inscription being
No. 336, Prosperum Iter Faciet.

319. Popvlis Expiatis   Leo XII
    For the people who were redeemed.
    A jubilee inscription.

320. Populis Immuni Emporio Donatis   Clement XII
    With the people having been given a free
    (tax-free) market.
    (See No. 458.)

321. Porta Aurea   Innocent XII
    Gate of gold.
    Used by Innocent XII, in addition to No.
    325, on jubilee issues.

322. Porta Coeli   Clement X
    Gate of Heaven.   Clement XII
    "How terrible is this place; this is no
    other but the House of God and the Gate
    of Heaven" (Gen. 28:17).
    (See Nos. 321 and 325.)

323. Portae Inferi Non Praevalebunt   Pius V
    "The gates of hell shall not prevail"   Innocent XI
    (Matt. 16:18).
    (See No. 274.)   Plate 5, No. 23.

324. Portam Sancta Clavsit—an Ivbelei
    He closed the Holy Door—in the Jubilee
    Year.
    On jubilee coins. Plate IX, No. 40.

325. PORTA PARADISI
      or
   PARADISI PORTA
   Gate of Paradise.
   (See Nos. 321 and 322.)

Innocent XII

326. POSSIDE SAPIENTIAM
   Acquire (get possession of) wisdom.
   "Get wisdom" (Prov. 4:5 and 16:16).

Innocent XI

327. P. P.
   Pater Patrum.
   Father of fathers.
   One of the titles of the pope formerly used on coins. It has appeared in this form at times since 1316 on coins of Pope John XXII, and as late as Alexander VI, in this form: Alexander P. P. VI. The most common title used on all papal coins is Pontifex Maximus, or its abbreviations, P. M., Pont. Max., Pont. M., etc. Other forms of the pope's title are Pap or Papa (on coins of Eugene IV), Pa (on coins of Nicholas V), etc.; while a purely temporal title is "The Lord____ P. P.," or, as shown on coins of Boniface VIII, Bo. PAPE DOMINE (The Lord Boniface—Pope). This form is still used by the present pope on many letters and documents: i.e. "Pius PP XII."
   (See No. 328.)

328. **P. P. P. P.**
   Pater Patrum Pater Pauperum.
   "Father of fathers, father of the poor."
   —a title first given to Pope Pelagius I (555–560) for his great charity.

Nicholas V,
after title
Calixtus III,
after title

329. PRAEOCCUPEMVS FACIEM EIVS   Innocent XII
     Let us come to Him without delay. (Lit-
     erally: Let us seek His face without de-
     lay.)
     Praeoccupemus faciem ejus in confes-
     sione: "Let us come to Him without
     delay, with praise" (Psalm 94:2).

330. PRAESIDIVM ET DECVS   Paul V to
     A protection and adornment.   Pius VI with
     This motto appeared on coins of the   a few excep-
     Bologna mint from 1620 to 1797, with   tions
     the exception of the years 1724 to 1740;
     a famous phrase applied by Horace to his
     patron Maecenas.

331. PRINCEPS APOSTOLORVM   Alexander VI
     Prince of Apostles (St. Peter).   and others
     Also shown PRINCEPES APOSTOLORVM.

332. PRINCIPES VRBIS PATRONI   Benedict XIV
     Princes, Patrons of the City.

333. PRO DEO UT ME DILIGERENT—ECCE   Clement VII
     HOMO
     "For God that they may love me—Be-
     hold the man!" (John 19:5).

334. PRODERIT IN TEMPORE   Benedict XIII
     It will be good in time of trouble.
     (See No. 140.)

335. PRO PRETIO ANIMAE   Innocent XI
     In price of a soul.
     "Nor the price of the redemption of his
     soul" (Psalm 48:9).

336. Prosperum Iter Faciet   Clement XI
    May He give a prosperous journey.
    "The Lord protecteth strangers [sojourn-
    ers or travelers]" (Psalm 145:9).
    (See No. 318.)

337. Pro Te Exorabit   Benedict XIII
    For you he will stretch forth (his hand).
    "Stretch forth thy hand to the poor"
    (Ecclus. 7:36).
    (See Nos. 235 and 306.)

338. Protege Roma   Sede vacante
    Rome, protect.   1644

339. Providentia   Julius III
    Providence.

340. Prudentia Pretiosior Est Argento   Clement XI
    "Wisdom is more precious than silver"
    (Prov. 16:16).

341. Prudentis Socia Fanvm   Gregory XIII
    Fano—companion of the prudent.
    A tribute to the city of Fano.

342. Publicae Utilitate   Sixtus IV
    For the public welfare.
    (See No. 433.)

343. Quaerite ut Abunditis   Clement XII
    Seek that ye may be enriched.
    "Ask, and it shall be given you; seek, and
    you shall find" (Matt. 7:7).
    (See No. 313.)

344. QUARE DUBITASTI   Clement VII
              or
       QUARE DUBITASTATIS   Calixtus III
       "Why have you hesitated?" (John 20:26–
       31).

345. QUI ACERVAT ALIIS CONGREGAT   Innocent XIII
       He who piles up for others gathers (for
       himself).
       (See No. 349.)

346. QUIA DOMINUS SUSCEPIT ME   Sede vacante
       Because the Lord hath helped me.   1623
       Misi quia Dominus adjuvit me: "Unless
       the Lord had helped me" (Psalm 93:17;
       also Psalm 117:13 and elsewhere).

347. QUI AURUM DILIGIT NON JUSTIFICA-   Clement XI
       BITUR
       He who loves money will not be justified
       (saved).
       (See No. 348.)

348. QUI CONFIDIT IN DIVITIIS CORRVET   Innocent XI
       He who trusts in riches will fall.
       "He that trusteth in his riches will fall"
       (Prov. 11:28).

349. QUI DAT PAUPERI NON INDIGEBIT   Innocent XI
       "He who gives to the poor will not go in
       want" (Prov. 28:27).
       (See No. 345.)

350. QUI DILIGVNT NOMEN TVVM   Urban VIII
       Who love Thy name.

"And all that love Thy name shall glory
in Thee" (Psalm 5:12).
(See No. 181.)

351. Quid Prodest Homini   Innocent XI
What doth it profit a man?
"For what shall it profit a man, if he gain
the whole world, and suffer the loss of
his soul?" (Mark 8:36.)

352. Quid Prodest Stulto   Innocent XI
What does it profit a fool?
"What doth it avail a fool to have riches
seeing he cannot buy wisdom?" (Prov.
17:16.)

353. Qui Ingreditvr Sine Macvla   Urban VIII
                    or
  Qui Ingre. Sine Macvla
He that walketh without stain.
"He that walketh without stain and
practiseth justice" (Psalm 142:2).
Also shown Qvi Ingreditv Sine
Macvla. Plate II, No. 10.

354. Qui Miseretur (Pauperi) Beatus Erit   Innocent XII
He who pities (the poor) will be blessed.   Clement XI
"He that hath mercy on the poor, lendeth
to the Lord, and He will repay him"
(Prov. 19:17).
(See No. 158.)

355. Quis Pauper? Avarus   Clement XI
Who is poor? The avaricious man.

356. Qui Videt Te Reddet Tibi   Innocent XII
"Who sees Thee, renders unto Thee"
(Luke 20:25).

357. Quod Habeo Tibi Do   Innocent XI
What I have I give thee.
"But he said to him: Son, thou art always
with me, and all I have is thine" (Luke
15:31).
"But Peter said: Silver and gold I have
none; but what I have I give thee" (Acts
3:6).

358. Radix Omnium Malorum   Innocent XI
The root of all evil.
"The desire for money is the root of all
evil" (I Tim. 6:10).

359. Redde Proximo in Tempore Suo   Clement XI
Give to thy neighbor in his need.

360. Re Frumentaria Restitvta   Alexander VIII
Restored supply of grain. Plate VI, No.
30.

361. Regina Pacis   Pius XI
Queen of Peace.
The Blessed Virgin.
Silver ten lire 1936, obverse: Pope's bust
left.
Reverse: Blessed Virgin with Christ
Child on throne. Regina Pacis on base
of throne.

362. RELIGIONE DEFENSA   Sede vacante
     Religion defended.   1800
     Referring to the occupation of Rome by
     the French.
     Obverse: Above inscription and bust of
     Blessed Virgin.
     Reverse: L'INCENDIO DI RONCIGLIONE—
     a view of burning city.
     (See No. 224.)

363. REPENTE DE COELO   Benedict XIV
     Suddenly from heaven.
     Referring to the descent of the Holy
     Ghost upon the Apostles.
     "Suddenly there came a sound from
     Heaven" (Acts 2:2). Plate XII, No. 57.

364. RERUM TIBI SUMMA POTESTAS   Julius III
     The greatest power of all is with thee.
     The testone bearing this inscription was
     issued on the double occasion of the
     jubilee of 1550 and the coronation of
     Julius III in St. Peter's, February 2, 1550.
     The obverse shows a variation of No. 105,
     IVLIO III P. M. DIVINITVS ELECTO A.
     IVBIL (Julius III, Pontifex Maximus,
     to one divinely chosen, in the jubilee
     year).

365. RESTITUTUISTI MAGNIFICENTIAM   Clement XI
     Thou hast restored the magnificence.
     Obverse: Papal arms.
     Reverse: View of Palace of Urbino.

366. RESTITUTUM COMMERC   Clement XI
     Commerce restored.
     (See No. 1.)   Plate X, No. 45.

367. REX REGUM DOMINUS DOMINI   Clement X
               or
     REX REG. DOMINUS DOM.
     "King of Kings, and Lord of Lords"
     (I Tim. 6:15).

368. ROGATE QVAE AD PACEM SVNT   Innocent XII
     Seek what is (beneficial) for peace.

369. ROMA CAPUT MUNDI—S.P.Q.R.   Senate of
     Rome, Capital of the World—the Senate   Rome (1099–
     and the Roman people.   1303)
                                              Martin V
                                              Eugene IV
                                              Calixtus III

370. ROMANA ECCLESIA   Nicholas V
     The Church at Rome.
     (See No. 371.)

371. ROMANÆ ECCLESIÆ FUNDATORES   Julius II
     Founders of the Church at Rome.
               or   Leo X
     RO. ECCL. FVDATORES
     (See No. 370.)

372. SACRIS DISPUNCTIONIBUS   Sixtus V
     For sacred accounting.
     Obverse: Papal arms.
     Reverse: An open book.

373. SACROS BASILIC LATERAN POSSES [1]   Clement IX

Possessor of the Holy Lateran Basilica.   Clement X

The Basilica of St. John Lateran is the   Clement XI
cathedral church of the pope, as bishop Clement XII
of Rome. "Lateran" is from the Roman Innocent X
family Lateranus, who originally had a   Innocent XII
palace on the present site of the Lateran Innocent XIII
Piazza. The palace was later a residence Alexander VIII
of the pope, now a museum. The Lat-   Benedict XII
eran Basilica was restored in the tenth
century by Pope Sergius III.

SACROSANC BASILIC LATERAN POSSES   Benedict XII

                                       Clement XIII

SACROSAN BASILIC LATERAN POSSESS   Pius VI

Plate VI, No. 29.   Pius VII

---

[1] At the solemn ceremonies on the date of the pope's taking possession of the cathedral church as bishop of Rome, money bearing this inscription was distributed to the poor. The popes who issued such coins, and the dates on which the ceremonies were held and the coins distributed, are shown below:

Clement IX: July 3, 1667.
Clement X: June 8, 1670.
Innocent XI: October 8, 1676.
Alexander VIII: October 23, 1689.
Innocent XII: April 13, 1692.
Clement XI: April 8, 1701.
Innocent XIII: November 16, 1721.
Benedict XIII: September 30, 1724.
Clement XII: November 19, 1730.
Benedict XIV: April 3, 1741—shown as SACROSANC, etc.
Clement XIII: November 12, 1758.
Pius VI: November 30, 1775. Shown as SACROSAN BASILIC. LATERAN POSSES on
    obverse; reverse, AVXILIVM DE SANCTO—1775.
Pius VII: November 20, 1801. Shown as SACR. BASILIC LATER. POSS. with QVATTR.
    (Quattrino.)

These were all minor coins, julios, double julios, quattrini, etc., for distribution to the poor. The same inscription was used but once on a two scudi gold piece by Innocent XII, which was not distributed.

    (See Cinagli: *Monete de' Papi*.)

374. SALVA NOS   Paul V
     Save us.
     "Lord, save me" (Matt. 15:30).

375. SALVA SCA CRUX   John XXII
     May the Holy Cross save.
     "Take up His cross and follow me"
     (Matt. 16:24).

376. SALVATOR MUNDI   Sixtus V
     "Saviour of the world" (John 4:42).

377. SANCTA DEI GENITRIX   Pius VI
     (Pray for us) Holy Mother of God.
     Hymn *"Salve Regina,"* composed in the
     year 1040 by a Benedictine monk. "The
     Angelus," etc.: *"Ora pro nobis, sancta
     Dei Genitrix."*

378. SANCTA ROMANA ECCLESIA   Nicholas V
     Holy Roman Church.

379. SANCTI BRUNONIS   Alexander VIII
     Of Saint Bruno.
     (See No. 96.)

380. SANCTIS SANCTA   Gregory XIII
     Holy of Holies—or the Most Holy Place.
     Cum Sancta sanctus eris (in various
     Psalms: 19:3; 21:4; etc.).

381. SANCTVS MATTHÆVS—APOSTOLVS   Innocent XI
     St. Matthew—Apostle.
     Silver scudo.
     Obverse: Bust of Pope right.

Reverse: St. Matthew writing at direction
of an angel.
Coined to commemorate the coronation
of Pope Innocent XI on the feast day of
St. Matthew. Plate V, No. 22.

382. SANCTVS PETRVS AP.   Innocent XI
St. Peter, Apostle.

383. SATIABOR GLORIA TVA   Clement X
I shall be filled with Thy glory.

384. SATIS AD NOCENDUM   Innocent XIII
Enough to do harm.

385. SCELERVM MATER AVARITIA   Clement VI
Avarice is the mother of crime.

386. SECTAMINI CHARITATEM   Innocent XIII
Pursue charity.

387. SECURITAS PAUPERUM   Sixtus V
The safety of the poor.

388. SEDEBIT IN PVLCHRITVDINE—PACIS   Innocent XII
Seated in the splendor (majesty) of peace.
(Cf. Matt. 25:31.)

389. SEDE VACANTE   Various pe-
With the Holy See vacant—during the   riods when
interregnum.   the Papal See
                                          was vacant

390. SEMPER OPERIBVS AVCTA   Gregory XIII
Always increased in work.
"Mighty in work" (Luke 24:19).

391. SEMPER SECUNDAE DOMINATOR ROMA   Alexander VII
Rome is always the mistress of prosperity.

392. SEQUERE ME   Gregory XIII
"Follow me" (Matt. 9:9 and 20:21).
(See No. 239.)

393. SERITE IN CHARITATE   Benedict XIII
Joined in charity.

394. (DIVITIAE) SI AFFLVANT NOLITE COR   Clement XI
APPONERE
If wealth flow in, set not your heart
thereon.
"If riches come, do not attach your heart
thereto" (Psalm 61:11).
(See Nos. 262 and 263.)

395. SIC DECET IMPLERE   Gregory XIII
"So it is fitting to fulfill" (Matt. 5:17–   Sixtus V
18).

396. SIC EXALTUS SANAT   Gregory XII
And so, lifted up, he heals.
"And I, if I be lifted up from the earth,
will draw all things to myself" (John
12:32).

397. SI ECCLESIAE RO.   John XXII
Seal (sigillo) of the Roman Church.

398. SIGNA INFIDELIBUS   Gregory XIII
A sign to the infidel.
Infidel: A word especially applied to the
Mohammedan.

399. SINE CLADE   Clement VII
Without slaughter.
Cessarit quassatio: "The slaughter
ceased" Deut. 32:26).
Commemorating the return of the duchy
of Ferrara to the Papal States.

400. S (ANCTA) MARIA ORA PR (O) NOB (IS)   Urban VIII
Holy Mary, Pray for us.
Prayer to the Blessed Virgin.

401. SOLA SUFFICIT   Gregory XIII
It (faith) alone is enough.   Sixtus V
Reverse design: Figure of Faith.

402. SOLATIVM MISERIS   Benedict XIII
Comfort for the sorrowful.
Litany of the Blessed Virgin Mary:
"Comforter of the afflicted." On January
12, 1728, Benedict XIII confirmed a
grant of an indulgence of two hundred
days to those reciting the Litany of the
Most Blessed Virgin.

403. SOLVIT ET LIGAT   Sixtus V
He binds and looses (Matt. 16:19).
(See Nos. 127 and 223.)

404. SPES NOSTRA   Innocent X
Our hope.
"Salve Regina": "Our life, our sweetness
and our hope."

405. S. PETRVS—FANVM FORTVNAE
St. Peter—the Temple of Fortune.
Fanvm Fortunae: the ancient name of

the city of Fano, so called because here
Julius Caesar had built his great Temple
of Fortune. This temple, turned into a
Christian church, is also commemorated
in the inscription COLONIA IVLIA FANES-
TRIS on coins of Sixtus V.

406. S. PETRVS—PRINC. APOST.   Innocent XI
St. Peter—Prince of the Apostles.
(See No. 382.)

407. SPIRITVS SANCTI MVNVS—   Sixtus V
The gift of the Holy Spirit.   Sede vacante
                                      1590

408. SPLENDET A MAJESTATE EJUS   Clement IX
"He is glorious with his majesty" (Matt.
25:31).

409. STATO CITTA DELLA VATICANO   Pius XI
State of Vatican City.   Sede vacante
Plate XVI.   1939
                    Pius XII

410. STATVIT SVPRA PETRAM PEDES MEAS   Sede vacante
And He set my feet upon a rock.   1621
"And he drew me forth from . . . the
slimy ooze and He set my feet upon a
rock" (Psalm 39:3).
(See No. 87.)

411. STELLA NOBIS EST ORTA   Gregory XIV
Our star is risen.
"For we have seen His star in the east"
(Matt. 2:2).
(See No. 4.)

412. SVBLIMIS INTER SIDERA
Sublime among the stars (Blessed Mother).

Clement X
Innocent XI

413. SUB TUUM PRAESIDIUM
Under thy protection.
A hymn to the Blessed Virgin: "We fly to thy protection," etc.
(See No. 414.)

Clement VII
Sixtus V
Clement VIII
and others

414. SUB TUUM PRAESIDIUM—CON (FVGIMVS)
Under thy protection—we take Refuge.
Commemorating the Immaculate Conception.

Urban VIII

415. SUB UMBRA MATRIS ECCLESIÆ
Under the shadow (protection) of Mother Church.

Clement VII

416. SVPER FVNDAMENTVM APOSTOLORVM
On the foundation of the Apostles.

Clement XI

417. SVPER HANC PETRAM
"Upon this rock" (Matt. 16:18).
(See Nos. 138 and 418.)

Gregory XIII

418. SVPRAM FIRMAM PETRAM
Upon a firm rock.
"Thou art Peter and upon this rock I shall build My church" (Matt. 16:18).
(See Nos. 138 and 417.) Plate XI, No. 52.

Clement XIII
Pius VII
Leo XII

419. SURGE TABITHA
Tabitha, arise!
"And they all being put forth, Peter

Gregory XIII

kneeling down prayed and turning to the
body, he said 'Tabitha arise' and she
opened her eyes and seeing Peter she sat
up" (Acts 9:40).
The reverse design refers to the miracle
of St. Peter.

420. SVSPICE ET VALEBIS   Gregory XIII
Look up and be strong.

421. TANQUAM LUTUM AESTIMABITUR   Innocent XII
He will be considered as dung (mud,
mire).
"They became as dung for the earth"
(Psalm 82:11).

422. TE MANE TE VESPERE   Urban VIII
Thou in the morning—Thou in the eve-
ning.
"Thine is the day, and thine is the night"
(Psalm 73:16).

423. TEMPERATO SPLENDEAT USU   Alexander VII
May it be glorious with temperate use.

424. THESAVRIZATE IN COELIS   Clement XIII
Lay up treasure in Heaven.
"Lay up to yourselves treasure in
Heaven; for where thy treasure is, there
is thy heart also" (Matt. 6:21).
(See No. 435.)

425. THESAVRVS INFINITVS   Gregory XIII
Infinite Treasure.   Gregory XIV

426. TIBI DOBO CLAVES REGIN   Benedict XIV
         also
     TIBI DABO CLA.   Sixtus V
     "I will give you the keys of the King-
     dom" (Matt. 16:19).
     (See Nos. 7 and 50.)

427. TOLLE ET PROIICE   Clement XII
     He raises and hurls away.
     (See Nos. 216 and 126.)

428. TOTA FORMOSA—FANVM   Clement VIII
     Complete beauty—Fano.

429. TOTA PULCHRA ES   Innocent XI
     Thou art all fair.
     "Thou art all fair, my love, and there is
     not a spot in thee" (Cant. 4:7).
     (See No. 232.)   Plate XII, No. 58.

430. TRAHE ME POST TE   Innocent XII
     Draw me close to Thee.
     "My soul hath stuck close to Thee"
     (Psalm 62:9).

431. TU AUTEM IDEM IPSE ES   Paul III
     But thou art always the selfsame.   Pius IV
     ". . . and Thy years shall not fail"
     (Psalm 101:28).
     Also on coins of Paul III, on which it is
     followed by ROMA—CAMERINI—MACER-
     (ATA) or RAVEN (NA), for the city at
     which the coins were issued.

432. **Tuis Precibus**   Gregory XIV
By thy prayers.
"It is therefore a holy and wholesome
thought to pray for the dead that they
may be loosed from sin" (II Macc.
12:16).

433. **Tvrem Tvere Pvblicam**   Gregory XVI
Do thou protect the public welfare.
(See No. 342.)

434. **Vbi Erant Sedentes**   Sede vacante
Where they were sitting.   1721
"And suddenly there came a sound from
Heaven as of a mighty wind coming, and
it filled the whole room where they were
sitting" (Acts 2:2).
The reverse design shows a radiant dove,
symbol of the Holy Ghost.

435. **Vbi Thesavrvs Ibi Co (r)**   Innocent XI
Where your treasure is, there your heart
will be.
"Lay up to yourselves treasure in Heaven;
for where thy treasure is, there is thy
heart also" (Matt. 6:21).
(See No. 424.)

436. **Vbi Vvlt Spirat**   Sede vacante
He breathes where He will (the Holy   1689
Spirit). Plate VI, No. 27.   1758

437. **Vmbram in Lvcem**   Clement XI
Light in darkness.
"To the righteous a light is risen up in
darkness" (Psalm 111:4).

438. Vna Est Colvmba Mea   Clement VIII
One is my dove.
"One is my dove, my perfect one is *but*
one" (Cant. 6:8).
Referring to the Holy Ghost.

439. Vnde Venit Avxilivm Mihi   Innocent X
              also
   Vnde Venit Avx Mihi
Whence comes my help.
Frequent in the scriptures.

440. Un Omnis Terra Adoret Me   Clement VII
All on earth adore Me.

441. Vnm Omnivm Votvm Salvs Principis   Benedict XIV
   —S.P.Q.B.
The safety of the prince is the one vow
(duty) of all—the Senate and the people
of Bologna.

442. Vnvs Sps et Vna Fides Erat in Eis   Clement VII
One hope and one faith was in them.
"That your faith and hope might be in
God" (I Peter 1:21).

443. Urbe Nobilitata   Clement XII
The noble City (Rome).

444. Urbe Restituta   Sixtus IV
The City (Rome) restored.

445. Vrbis Parme Secvritas   Adrian VI
Security of the people at Parma.

446. VT ABVNDENTIS MAGIS   Clement X
     That you may abound the more.
     "May the Lord multiply you and make
     you abound in charity" (I Thess. 3:12).

447. VT ALAT EOS IN FAME   Benedict XIV
     That He may feed them in the famine.
     "To deliver their souls from death; and
     feed them in famine" (Psalm 32:19).

448. VT DETVR   Innocent XII
     That it may be given.

449. VTERE QVASI HOMO FRVGI   Clement XIII
     Use the food like a man.
     (*Cf.* Exod. 16.)

450. VT FACIANT IVSTIAS ET ELEEMOSYN   Clement XI
     That justice and alms (charity) may be
     extended.

451. VT NON DEFICIAT   Gregory XIII
     That it may not fail.
     (See No. 270.)

452. VT SALVI FIANT   Clement XIII
     That they may be saved.

453. VADO ET VENIO AD VOS   Sede vacante
     I go and I will come to you.   1700

454. VÆ VOBIS DIVITIBVS   Clement XIII
     Health to you in abundance.
     (See No. 457.)

455. Væ Vobis Qvi Satvrati Estis   Clement XII
     Health to you who are filled.

456. Vanvm Est Vobis   Clement XII
     It is useless for you.
     (*Cf.* Mark 8:36.)

457. Vas Electionis   Paul V
     Vessel of election (St. Paul).
     Cf. Acts 9:15.
     (See No. 301.)

458. Vectigalibvs Remissis   Alexander VIII
     Freed from taxes (Literally: With taxes
     remitted).
     Speaking of Christ: "He is free from the
     duty of Temple Tribute" (Matt. 17:
     24–5.
     (See No. 320.)

459. Vene et Mare Obedivnt Ei   Innocent XI
     "The winds and the seas obey him"
     (Matt. 8:27).

460. Veni Lvmen Cordivm   Sede vacante
     Come, O Light of Hearts.   1774
     Referring to the Holy Ghost.   1830

461. Veni Sancte Spiritis   Sede vacante
     Come, Holy Spirit.   1740
     Cum Sancto, Sanctus, etc. (Psalm 17:26).   1769
     Plate XIII, No. 60.

462. Vente ad Me Omnes et Ego Reficiam   Pius V
     Vos   Gregory XIII

Come to me, all of you, and I will refresh   Sixtus V
you.

463. VERA REDEMPTIO FIDA PROTECTIO   Clement VII
Truth redeems, faith protects.
On coins issued at the Parma mint.

464. VIATORI PATET   Benedict XIV
The way lies open for the traveler.
On a jubilee issue.

465. VIA VERITAS ET VITA   Julius III
"I am the way, the truth and the life"
(John 14:6).
(See No. 121.)

466. VICIT LEO DE TRIBV IVDA   Leo X
"The Lion of the Tribe of Juda has con-
quered" (Rev. 5:5).

467. VICTORIA DNN   Adrian I
Victory of the lords.
The first inscription of historical significance used on papal coins. Shown on a
denaro variously ascribed to Constantinople (CONOB) and Rome (R. M.:
Romana Moneta).

468. VIDEANT PAVPERES ET LAETENTVR   Innocent XI
"Let the poor see and rejoice" (Psalm   Clement XI
68:33).

469. VIDERVNT OCVLI MEI SALVTARE TVVM   Clement XI
Mine eyes have seen Thy salvation.
"Because my eyes have seen Thy salva-
tion" (Luke 2:30).

470. Vindica D. Sangvin Nrm Qvi Pro Te   Pius II
   Effvsvs Est
   Avenge, O Lord, our blood which is shed
   for Thee.
   "How long, O Lord, dost Thou not judge
   and revenge our blood on them that
   dwell on the earth?" (Rev. 6:10).

471. Virgo Clemens   Clement VIII
   Clement Virgin.
   O clemens, O pia, O dulcis Virgin Maria:
   "O clement, O loving, O sweet Virgin
   Mary" (hymn *"Salve Regina"*).
   Clement VIII in 1601 forbade any prayer
   other than the Litany of the Blessed Vir-
   gin Mary to be said in public prayer.

472. Virgo Concipiet   Alexander VII
   A virgin shall conceive.
   "A virgin shall conceive and bring forth
   a son whose name shall be called Eman-
   uel" (Isa. 7:14).
   The reverse design shows the Blessed
   Virgin.

473. Virgo Faveas Parmae Tvae   Julius II
   Virgin, protect thy Parma.
   Coins issued at Parma.

474. Virgo Tva Gloria Partvs   Julius III
   Virgin, thy glory is birth.   Paul III
                                            Gregory XIII

475. Vivit Devs   Urban VIII
   The Lord liveth.
   Vivet Dominus, et benedictus Deus

meus: "The Lord liveth, and blessed be
my God" (Psalm 17:47; 23:7; etc.) . Plate
II, No. 11.

476. Vox de Throno Basilic Liber [1] F. seva   Clement XI
Voice from the throne of the Basilica of
Liberius.
This is the basilica of the pope—the pres-
ent Church of Mary Major. Thus the in-
scription means freely: "The voice from
the throne of the pope."
F. Seva: Engraver.
Obverse: Bust of Pope.
Reverse: Pope on St. Peter's chair point-
ing to an open book—thirteen figures.

477. Vvltvs Sanctvs   Julius III
        also
Vvltvs Sanc. or Vvltvs S. Alma Ro.
Sacred countenance.
Lumen vultus tui: "The light of Thy
countenance" (Psalm 4:7) .

---

[1] Vox de Throno in exergue. Basilic Liber on base of altar.

Emperors and Other Rulers, Temporal and Ecclesiastical, Mentioned on Papal Coins

In the beginning it was customary to show the name of the pope and the emperor. The earliest papal grosso, that of Leo III (795–816), shows on reverse: CARLVS IPA, for Charlemagne Emperor, who ruled from 800 to 814, and LODICHVS IPA, Louis I (of Aquitaine) Emperor (813–840), son of Charlemagne.

Louis I is also shown on the grosso of Stephen V (816–817) as LVDOVVICVS IMP or LVDOVVICVS IMP PIVS.

Louis I appears also with Paschal I (817–824) as LVDOVVICVS IMP ROMA, and with Eugene II (824–827) and Valentine (827), as well as with Gregory IV (827–844), on the coins of the latter as LVDOVVICVS IMP PP (*Perpetuo et Perpertuus*) PIVS.

Gregory IV also shows HLOTHARIVS IMP PIVS for Lothaire, a descendant of Charlemagne, who reigned from 840 to 855, and the same inscription is used on coins of Sergius II (844–847), who also is shown with Louis, son of Lothaire who was crowned emperor by Sergius, as LODOVVICVS IP PIVS.

Benedict III (855–858) appears with Lothaire and Louis, the latter being Louis II, a descendant of Charlemagne, who reigned from 855 to 875, and also is mentioned on coins of Nicholas I, the Great (858–867), Adrian II (867–872), and John VIII (872–882).

Marinus I (882–884) shows on his coins CAROLVS IPAR for Carloman of Bavaria or Charles the Bald of France, both descendants of Charlemagne, the latter crowned emperor by John VIII in 875 and the former in 880. Carloman is also mentioned with Adrian II (884–885) and Stephen VI (885–891).

Formosus (891–896) appears with VVIDO IMP ROMA for Guido (Guy) III of Spoleto, who reigned from 891 to 894.

Stephen VII, (896–897; some call this pope Stephen VI and

disregard the claims of the former Stephen VI) shows LANVERTO for Lambert, son of Guido, who was crowned emperor by Formosus. Stephen VII also shows ARNOLFVS for Arnulf, king of Germany, who disputed the title and forced Lambert to retire to Spoleto. Arnulf was then crowned emperor by the pope. Later Lambert returned to Rome as emperor and his name again appears on coins of the popes with those of Romanus I (897–898), as well as on those of Theodore II (898).

Benedict IV (900–903) issued coins bearing the name of LODOVIC for Louis of Provence, who was crowned emperor by this pope. However, Louis was captured by his rival, Berengarius, king of Italy (who reigned as emperor from 897 to 915), Louis being blinded by Berengarius and banished from Italy. The coins of John X (914–928) are inscribed BERNEGARIV for Berengarius.

The coins of Agapitus II (946–955) have the letters ALBR for Alberic, who died in 954. Alberic was the brother of John X and both were sons of Marozia, daughter of Theodora and Theophylact. Marozia later married Hugh of Pavia, king of Italy. Alberic imprisoned his mother and defeated Hugh, and his soldiers sacked and pillaged Rome.

John XII (956–964) issued a denaro showing the words DOMVS IOHA PAPA or DOM IOANES PAPA on the obverse and OTTO IMPERATO on the reverse, meaning "The Lord John, Pope," and "Emperor Otto I," King of Italy, respectively.

Benedict V (965) is also shown with Otto, while Benedict VI (972-973) appears with OTTO IMPERATO for Otto II, son of Otto I. John XIV (985) issued coins with OTTONI IMPERATOR for Otto III.

Leo IX (1049–1054) is shown with HENRICVS IMP ROMANORV for Henry III, emperor of Germany, and later emperor of Rome. Leo IX himself was a German, born Bruno, later bishop of Toul.

The times of Leo IX may be considered as a period when the

glory of the Church dominated the whole known world. This pope lived in the time of William the Conqueror, Edward the Confessor of England, and Macbeth, king of Scotland.

Beginning with Paschal II (1099) and continuing through the pontificate of Benedict XI (1303), the mint at Rome was controlled by the Senate of Rome. On resumption of coining by the popes with Boniface VII (1294–1303), rulers were not shown on the coins, with a few exceptions as noted:

On the julio of John XXIII (1410–1415) appears LADISLAVS REX ET C and the arms of Ladislaus, king of Sicily.

While the coins of the antipopes are not embraced in this study, one of particular interest must be mentioned, that issued for Antipope Felix V (1439–1449), which shows on obverse AMEDEVS COM FERT and reverse DE SABAVDIA. The former is the insignia of the Visconti family of Milan and is ascribed by Cinagli, quoting Bellini, to Philip M. Visconti, duke of Milan. Cinagli also mentions that it is also attributed to Amedeo VIII, duke of Savoy, who was Antipope Felix V, and further states that the legend is part of the insignia of the house of Savoy and that FERT means FORTITVDO EJVS RHODVM TENVIT (His bravery held Rhodes.)

It is interesting to note that the present arms of the Italian ruling family of the house of Savoy include the word *fert,* which also means "strength" in Italian.

Duke Varano of Camerino is honored on money coined at Camerino by Leo X, the reverse of the coins reading Io MARIA CAMERINI DVX. The title on the obverse is also interesting: LEO X PONT MAX DECORAVIT (Noble) or the same and CVLTVI (Teacher).

Included in coins of Gregory XIII (1572–1585) is that issued for Henry III, king of France, inscribed HENRICVS III D. G. FRAN ET. P. REX—1583.

For a time it became the custom to issue certain coins in honor of the pope's cardinal legate, or personal ambassador.

The first of these, issued for Pius V and Julius III, bear the legend ALEX FAR C LEGA AVE or ALEX FARN LEGAT AVE, for Cardinal Alexander Farnese, cardinal legate at Avignon.

Paul II continued the practice and issued a grosso with S. PAVLVS MACR and CAR. S ANG M L, referring to St. Paul of Macerata and Ranucius, "Cardinal Sant' Angeli Marchiae Legatus."

Leo X issued like coins for Cardinal Nicoli Fieschi.

Pius IV and St. Pius V, as well as Sixtus V, honored Cardinal Carlo Bourbon with scudi d'oro showing CARO CARD D BOURBON LEGAT AVENIONEN, KA DE BOURBON LEGAT AVENIONEN, and CARO C. DE BOURBON LEGAT AVENIO respectively.

Gregory XIII issued scudi with CARO CAR LEG GEOR CAR COLLE AV for the cardinals legate Borbone and Conti.

Clement VIII issued an eight scudi d'oro with OCT CARD DE AQVAVIVA LEG AVEN 1596, and a double scudo d'oro of the same year for Octavio Acquaviva, cardinal legate at Avignon.

Clement VIII also issued a double scudo d'oro dated 1600 with CAROL DE COMITIBVS EPS ANCON PROLEG AVEN for Cardinal Conti, the prolegate, and a julio for 1593 with SIL SABELLVS VICE LEGA AVEN for Cardinal Silvio Savelli, vice-legate at Avignon for the years 1592–3. This pope also issued a quattrino for Cardinal Pietro Aldobrandini, first cardinal legate for Ferrara, inscribed PETRVS ALDOBRAN (or ALDOBRANDINVS) FERRARIAE LEG.

On gold and silver scudi and various testones of Paul V are found the inscription SCIP BVRGHESIVS CARD LEG. AVEN, or SCIPI BVRGHESIVS CARD LEG AVEN. for Cardinal Scipione Borghesi, papal legate at Avignon from 1605 to 1621. Testones of this pope for 1612 and 1613 show PHILONARD CARD P. LEG. AVEN or PHILIP PHILONARD CARD P. LEG. AVEN, PHIS RE CARD, or PHILONARDVS P. LEG AVEN. for Cardinal Filippo Filonard, prolegate at Avignon 1610–1614.

Eight scudi d'oro and silver scudi of Gregory XV (1621–1623) bear the legend LVD CARD LVDOVISIVS CAMER LEG AVEN for Cardinal Ludovisi, papal legate at Avignon.

The julio of sede vacante 1623 shows on the obverse Iocobvs Serra Leg Sed V and reverse Civitas Ferrariae for Cardinal Jacob Serra, papal legate at Ferrara.

Urban VIII issued coins reading Franciscvs Card Barberinvs Leg Aven for Cardinal Francisco Barberini, legate at Avignon 1623–1633, and other gold scudi with Antonivs Card Barber-invs Leg Ave for Antonio Barberini, papal legate at Avignon 1633–1644, both nephews of Urban VIII (Maffeo Barberini). Quattrini of this pope for 1635 and 1636 show Ant. Car Bar. Le. Ave and silver scudi show on the obverse Vrbanvs VIII Pont Max An XII Gas. Mol., the latter two words for Gaspare Mola, papal engraver.

Innocent X issued coins for Antonivs Card. Barberinvs in 1644 and others for Cardinal Camillo Panfili, cardinal legate for the pope at Avignon from 1644 to 1650, inscribed Camillivs Card Pamphilivs Legat Aven. Cardinal Panfili was related to Innocent X (John Baptist Panfili).

Alexander VII showed the inscription Flavivs Card Ghisivs Legat Aven for Cardinal Flavio Chigi, papal legate at Avignon 1657–1668, and, on the obverse of the carlini of 1660, 1662, 1665, and 1666, Flavivs Card Ghisivs Lega Ave. The reverse read Pax Orietur Ex Montibus, not showing the pope's name. Another coin of this period which shows the cardinal legate's name but omits any reference to the pope is the grosso of 1658 inscribed Flavivs Card. Ghisivs Legat Ave on the obverse and Semper Secundae Dominator Romae on the reverse.

Innocent VII issued grossi with the legend Petrvs Card Otthobonvs Legat, and one simply inscribed P. C. L., for Cardinal Peter Otthobonus, papal legate at Avignon.

Saints, Apostles, the Blessed Virgin, and the Holy Ghost Honored in Inscriptions

SS Peter and Paul, sometimes together and sometimes separately, are the earliest mentioned saints on papal coins, and are by far the most frequent. St. Peter and St. Paul are the special protectors of Rome and coins of the Rome mint show their names from the earliest times to the present. St. Peter is mentioned as S. PETRVS, SAN PETRVS, SANCTVS PETRVS, and in many other ways. St. Paul is generally shown as S. PAVLVS. When both of these saints are mentioned on the earliest coins they are shown as S. PE—S. PA.

Many other saints, of course, are mentioned on papal coins. St. Thomas is shown on coins of Parma as SANCTVS THOMAS or as DIVO THOME.

After St. Peter and St. Paul, St. Frances of Rome is inseparably connected with Rome as the patroness of the Eternal City. She was born in Rome in 1384 and died in 1440. However, she is honored on papal coins only once, by St. Pius V, with obverse ECCLESIA and reverse S FRAN PROT ME (St. Frances, protect me).

St. George, either alone or with St. Maurelius, is mentioned as the protector of Ferrara, St. Ubaldus as the protector of Gubbio, St. Hilary or St. John as protector of Parma. SS Venantius and Ansovino are shown as protectors of Camerino, St. Paternia as protector of Fano, St. Lawrence as protector of Viterbo, St. Antoninus as protector of Placentia, St. Petronius as protector of Bologna, St. Apollinaris as protector of Ravenna, St. Gemianus as protector of Modena, St. Felicianus as protector of Foligno, and St. Julian and St. Cyriacus as protectors of Macerata.

Some saints have been honored in designs of papal coins: St. Thomas of Villanova, Saint Lawrence, St. Luke shown with the

Blessed Virgin, St. Pius V shown on the occasion of his beatification. St. Veronica is honored on the design of the zecchino of Paul II, with the inscription ALMA ROMA, and also on coins of Gregory XIII, with the inscription IMAGO SALVTVS. St. Francis of Assisi is honored in the design of coins of Sixtus V, where he is shown receiving the stigmata. The Saviour is honored often in designs, one occasion being on the gold scudo of Julius III, with the inscription VIA VERITAS ET VITA. St. Matthew writing his gospel is shown in the design of the scudo of Innocent XI; St. Michael the Archangel is honored in the design of the scudo of Urban VIII, twelfth year. Special events are honored and depicted in designs at times, such as the coming of the Magi on the two zecchini piece of Leo X with the inscription LVX VERA IN TENEBRIS LUCET, and the finding of the child Jesus in the temple on the fifty baiocchi of Gregory XVI with the inscription LVMEN AD REVELATIONEM GENTIVM.

The Blessed Virgin Mary is commemorated frequently in the inscriptions shown on papal coins. Now and then the Blessed Virgin is honored in designs of coins without inscriptions referring to her, such as in certain coins of Fano with the legend FANVM FORTVNAE and the three baiocchi copper coin of sede vacante 1799, FEDELTA E RELIGIONE. In the inscriptions mentioned elsewhere the Blessed Virgin is commemorated or called upon for help as follows:

AVE GRATIA PLENA
AVE MARIA
CANDOR LUCIS AETERNAE
CAVSA NRAE LAETITIAE
DILEXI DECOREM DOMVS TVAE
ET MERITAS EXALTATO
FORE TVTVM PRAESIDIVM
FUNDA NOS IN PACE
ITER PARA TUTUM
MACULA NON EST IN TE

Monstra Te Esse Matrem
Praesidivm et Decvs
Protege Roma
Regina Pacis
Religione Defensa
Sancta Dei Genitrix
Solativm Miseris
Spes Nostra
Svblimis inter Sidera
Sub Tuum Praesidium
Tota Pulchra Es
Virgo Clemens
Virgo Concipiet
Virgo Faveas Parmae Tvae
Virgo Tva Gloria Partvs

The Holy Ghost is often the subject of prayer or supplication and is called upon in the inscriptions shown, as follows:

Accende Lvmen Sensibvs
Beati Qvi Cvstodivnt Vias Meas
Coronat Te in Misericordia
Dabitvr Vobis Paraclitvs
Da Quieta Tempora
Da Recta Sapere
Docebit et Svggeret
Emitte Coelitvs Lvcis Tvae Radivm
Emitte Spiritvm Tvvm
Illuminet Corda Nostra
Illuxit Illucescat Adhuc
Infunde Amorem Cordibus
In Ipso Edocti Estis
Non Relinquam Vos Orphanos
Non Vos Relinquam Orphanos
Nutantia Corda in Direges
Paraclitus Illuminet

PATER QUI MISIT ME TRAHET EVM
REPENTE DE COELO
SPIRITVS SANCTI MVNVS
VBI ERANT SEDENTES
VBI VVLT SPIRAT
VNA EST COLVMBA MEA
VADO ET VENIO AD VOS
VENI LVMEN CORDIVM
VENI SANCTE SPIRITIS

War and peace, concordats and peace treaties are the subjects of many inscriptions, as follows:

AD PATRIAM REDII
BELLVM CONTERAM DE TERRA
COGENTE INOPIA REI FRVMENTARIAE
COGITO COGITATIONES PACIS
CONCORDIA ALMA ROMA
CONFREGIT POTENTIAS ARCVVM
DA PACEM DOMINE IN DIEBVS NOSTRIS
DA QUIETA TEMPORA
DELECTABITVR IN MVLTITVDINE PACIS
DEVS PACIS CONTERET SATANAM
DIGNVS VICTORIAM
DONA NOBIS PACEM
EX COLLATO ÆRE DE REBVS SACRIS ET PROPHANIS IN EGE-
    NORVM SVBSIDIVM
EX MONTIBVS PAX ORIETVR
EXVRGAT D ET DISSIPENTVR INIMICI EJVS
EXVRGAT DEVS
FACTVS EST IN PACE LOCVS EJVS
FIAT PAX
FIAT PAX IN VIRTUTE TUA
FIAT PAX SUPER ISRAEL
IN HOC SIGNO VINCES
IPSE EST PAX NOSTRA

LEGIONE AD BELLUM SACRUM INSTRUCTA
MELIORA MANENT
NON EST PAX
NUNTIA PACIS
OPVS JVSTITIAE PAX
ORATIONE ET IEIVNIO—DEO EXERCITVVM
PACEM LOQUETUR GENTIBUS
PACEM MEAM DO VOBIS
PACI PONTIFICIÆ
PAX DEI CUSTODIAT CORDA VESTRA
PAX ORIETVR EX MONTIBVS
PAX ROMANA
P. C. I. R. C.—*Pax Christi in Regno Christi*
ROGATE QVAE AD PACEM SVNT
SEDEBIT IN PVLCHRITVDINE—PACIS
SINE CLADE
VNVM OMNIVM VOTVM SALVS PRINCIPIS

Charity, greed, and avarice are the subjects of a good many inscriptions. The ones appearing in the list in this volume are shown below:

AERVGO ANIMI CVRA PECVLII
ALIIS DIVES
AVARVS NON IMPLEBITVR
BEATI PAVPERES
BEATVS QVI INTELLIGIT SVPER EGENVM
BENEFAC HUMILI
CONTEMPTA PECVNIA DITAT
CRESCENTEM SEQUITUR CURA PECUNIAM
CUM EGENIS
DA ET ACCIPE
DA PAUPERI
DAT ACCIPIT REDDIT
DATE ET DABITVR
DAT IN PRETIVM

DAT OMNIBVS AFFLVENTER
DEDIT PAVPERIBVS
DELICTA OPERIT CHARITAS
DEUS CHARITAS EST
DEUS DAT OMNIBUS AFFLUENTER ET NON IMPROPERAT
DISPERSIT DEDIT PAVPERIBVS
DIVES IN HVMILITATE
EDENT PAVPERES ET SATVRABVNTVR
EGENO ET PAVPERI
EGENO SPES
ELEVAT PAVPERVM
ESAVRIENTES IMPLEBO
FACIANT IVSTITIAS ELEEMOSYN
FER AVXILIVM
FERRO NOCENTIVS AVRVM
FOENERATVR DOMINO QVI MISERETVR PAVPERI
FOENVS PECVNIÆ FVNVS EST ANIMÆ
HABETIS PAVPERIS
IN CIBOS PAVPERVM
IN EGENOS
INOPIÆ SIT SUPPLEMENTUM
MANVM TVAM APERVIT INOPE
MULTOS PERDIDIT ARGENTUM
MULTOS PERDIDIT AURUM
NEQUE DIVITIAS
NOLI AMARE NE PERDAS
NOLI COR APPONERE
NOLI LABORARE UT DITERIS
NOLITE THESAURIZARE
NON CONCUPISCES ARGENTUM
NON IN AVARITIAM
NOVIT JVSTVS CAVSAM PAVPERVM
NULLUS ARGENTO COLOR EST AVARIS
OCULI EJUS IN PAUPEREM
PAUPERI PORRIGE MANUM TUAM

PECCATA ELEEMOSYNIS REDIME
PETENTI TRIBVE
PRO TE EXORABIT
QUI ACERVAT ALLIS CONGREGAT
QUI AURUM DILIGIT NON JUSTIFICABITUR
QUI CONFIDIT IN DIVITIIS CORRVET
QUI DAT PAUPERI NON INDIGEBIT
QUI MISERETUR BESTUS ERIT
QUIS PAUPER? AVARUS
RADIX OMNIUM MALORUM
REDDE PROXIMO IN TEMPORE SUO
SCELERVM MATER AVARITIA
SECTAMINI CHARITATEM
SECURITAS PAUPERUM
SERITE IN CHARITATE
SI AFFLVANT NOLITE COR APPONERE
THESAVRIZATE IN COELIS
VT ALAT EOS IN FAME
VT DETVR
VT FACIANT IVSTIAS ET ELEEMOSYN
VIDEANT PAVPERES ET LAETENTVR

Inscriptions having to do with faith are fairly numerous:

AB STELLA LVX ORITVR
ABVNDET IN GLORIAM DEI
AETERNA SALVS
AGGREGATO RELIGIO
AVDI DOMINE ET MISERERE
AUXILIUM DE SANCTO
BEARE SOLEO AMICOS MEOS
BENED. VOS OMNI DEVS
CONSERVATÆ PEREVNT
CUM EXULTATIONE
CUNCTIS SPRETIS TE SOLAM
CURABANTUR OMNES

Dabis Discernere Inter Malvm et Bonvm
Dabit Frvctvm Svvm in Tempore
Dedit Pignvs
Defluit et Influit
De Lvto Fæcis
Dirige Dne Gressvs Nros
Dispersa Congregat
Divites in Virtvte
Ecce Agnvs Dei
Ecce Fides
Ego Sum Lux Mundi
Ego Sum Via Veritas et Vita
Egrediatvr Popvlvs et Colligat
Et Morientvr in Siti
Fedelta e Religione
Fixa Manebit
Foedvs Est inter Me et Te
Gens et Regnum Quod Non Servierit Tibi Peribit
Gloria in Excelsis Deo
Gratia Dei Omne Bonum
Haec Avtem Qvæ Parasti Cvivs Ervnt
Hinc Fides et Fortitvdo
Hodie Salvs Facta Est Mvndo
(Hominibvs Volvntatis) Qvi Diligvnt Nomen Tvvm
I. E. M. I. S. S.—*Ivstitia Eivs Manet in Secvla Secvlorvm*
In Omnis Terra Adoret Me
In Te Domine Speravi
In Te Signum Nostrae Redemptionis
In Te Sitio
In Verbo Tvo
In Via Virtvtis
Lumen Semitis Meis
Luminaria Verae Fidei
Lux Mundi
Lux Vera in Tenebris Lucet

Me Sequere
Misit D. Ang. Svvm et Liberavit Me
Modice Fidei Qvare Dvbitatis Dominvs
Mortifera Non Nocebvnt
Ne Forte Offendiculum Fiat
Ne Proiicias Me in Tempore Senectutis
Noli Anxius Esse
Non Aliunde Salus
Non Apparentium Est Fides
Non Aurum Sed Nomen
Non Deficiet Fides
Nostra Redemptio
Nunquam Deficiet
Nunquam Sitiet
Pro Deo ut Me Diligerent
Pro Pretio Animae
Prosperum Iter Faciet
Quare Dubitasti
Quia Dominus Suscepit Me
Qui Diligvnt Nomen Tvvm
Salva Nos
Salva Sca Crux
Salvator Mundi
Satiabor Gloria Tva
Sequere Me
Sic Decet Implere
Sic Exaltus Sanat
Signa Infidelibus
Sola Sufficit
Svspice et Valebis
Te Mane Te Vespere
Thesavrvs Infinitvs
Trahe Me Post Te
Tu Autem Idem Ipse Es
Tuis Precibus

VNDE VENIT AVXILIVM MIHI
UN OMNIS TERRA ADORET ME
VNVS SPS ET VNA FIDES ERAT IN EIS
VT NON DEFICIAT
VT SALVI FIANT
VENE ET MARE OBEDIVNT EI
VENTE AD ME OMNES ET EGO REFICIAM VOS
VERA REDEMPTIO FIDA PROTECTIO
VIA VERITAS ET VITA
VIDERVNT OCVLI MEI SALVTARE TVVM
VIVIT DEVS
VVLTVS SANCTVS

The inscriptions issued in special honor of churches, cities, and saints are shown below:

ALMA ROMA
APOSTOLORVM PRINCEPS
BEATO PIO V
DIE NAT SS MAGNI ET OP EP BRUNONSIS ANACHOR
DIVO THOME or SANCTVS THOMAS
GENVS ALTO A SANGUINE
IN HONOREM S. THEODORI MAR.
PRINCEPS APOSTOLORVM
PRINCIPES VRBIS PATRONI
PRUDENTIS SOCIA FANVM
ROMA CAPUT MUNDI—S.P.Q.R.
SANCTI BRUNONIS
SANCTVS MATTHÆVS—APOSTOLVS
SANCTVS PETRVS AP
S. PETRVS—FANVM FORTVNAE
S. PETRVS—PRINC APOST
VRBIS PARME SECVRITAS

Commerce, public works, and monuments are the subjects of a few inscriptions:

A. A. A. F. F.—*Restitvtvm Commerc*
COMMODITAS VIARVM REDVX
DECVS PATRIÆ
FONTIS ET FORI ORNAMEN
LEVATA ONERE PATRIA
PATRIE ET SCIENTARIVM INSTITVTO MAGNIFICE AVCTO SPQB
PATRI PATRIAE
PONS CIVITA CASTELLANAE
POPULIS IMMUNI EMPORIO DONATIS
PUBLICAE UTILITATE
RE FRUMENTARIA RESTITVTA
RESTITUTUISTI MAGNIFICENTIAM
RESTITVTVM COMMERC
SEMPER SECVNDAE DOMINATOR ROMA
TVREM TVERE PVBLICAM

The apostolic succession or the authority of the popes and the Church, spiritual and temporal, are mentioned in inscriptions as follows:

ACCIPE CLAVES REGNI COELORVM
APOSTOLORVM PRINCEPS
AVCTA AD METAVRVM DITION
BON. P. IVL A TYRANNO LIBERAT
DIVINITVS ELECTO
ECCLESIAE RAVENNA
ECCLESIAE RO. FUNDATORES
ECCLESIA ROMANA
ET IN COELIS ERIT LIGATVM
ET SUPER HANC PETRAM
ET TIBI DABO CLAVES
FUNDATORES ROMAN ECCLESIAE
FUNDATORI ECCLESIAE
GLORIOSI PRINCIPES
GLORIOSI PRINCIPES TERRAE

In Omnem Terram Exivit Sonus Corum
Isti Sunt Patres Tui Verique Pastores
Libertas Ecclesiasticus
Ligat et Solvit
Navis Aeternae Salutis
Non Praevalebunt
Pastor Doctor
Pastori et Principi Senatus Bononiensis
Pastori Ovium Vas Electi
Petre Ecce Templum Tuum
Petre Pasce Oves Meas
Pe (trus) Ap (osto) lvs Pav (lvs) Doc (tor) Gentivm
P. P.—*Pater Patrum*
P. P. P. P.—*Pater Patrum Pater Pauperum*
Religione Defensa
Romana Ecclesia
Romanæ Ecclesiæ Fundatores
Sacrosanc Basilic Lateran Possess
Sancta Romana Ecclesia
Si Ecclesiae Ro.
Solvit et Ligat
Svper Fvndamentvm Apostolorvm
Svper Hanc Petram
Svpram Firmam Petram
Tibi Dabo Claves Regin
Vas Electionis
Vox de Throno

Jubilee inscriptions follow the same general pattern, i.e. a
reference to the Porta Sancta, or Holy Door, or an allusion to remission of sins. They are easily recognizable, but for con-
venience are enumerated below:

Absolvto an Ivbilei
Accipivnt Remissionem
Anno Ivbelei

Anno Propitationis
Anno Remissionis
Aperiet Dnus Thesavrvm Svvm
Aperivt Cvnctvs Apostolor. Princeps
Apervit et Clavsit
Clavsis Foribvs Veniet et Dabit Pacem
Clavsit Anno Ivbilei
Dedi Corem Te Ostium
Diligit Dnvs Portas Sion
Divinitvs Electo
Et Clavsit
Et Clavso Ostio Ora Patrem Tvvm
Et in Coelis Erit Ligatvm
Et Janvas Coeli Apervit
Et Portae Coeli Apertae Svnt
Haec Porta Domini
In Portas Opera Ejus
Iusti Intrabunt in Eam
Ivstis Patet
Ivstitiae Pacisque Cvlt
Ivstitia Resvrgens
Mundi Revertvntvr
Ob Sanctificationem Ivbilei
Ostivm Coeli Apertvm in Terris
Peccata Redime
Pietatis Vitaeque
Popvlis Expiatis
Porta Aurea
Porta Coeli
Portae Inferi Non Praevalebunt
Porta Paradisi
Portam Sancta Clavsit
Qui Ingreditvr Sine Macvla
Rerum Tibi Summa Potestas
Viatori Patet

Papal Engravers, Die Sinkers, Mint Masters, and Directors, and Their Signatures on Coins

A. B.: See Bellagrandi, Agostino. The signature A. B. also appears on coins of the Bologna mint issued for Popes Innocent XIII and Benedict XIII. The engraver of these coins is unidentified by Cinagli or *Corpus nummorum Italicorum,* but in all probability was Antonio Maria Beneventi, engraver at Modena and elsewhere.

A. C.: See Corsolini, Andrea, and Cesari, Alessandro.

A. H.: See Hameran: Alberto Hamerani.

Andra, Giovanni, engraver at Rome for Innocent XI and Alexander VIII. His signature, G. A. L., appears on medals, but no coins seem to show this.

A. P. or A. P. P: See Perpenti, Andronica. Ap on other coins refers to *Apostolus,* generally shown with St. Peter.

A. S.: See Segni, Antonio. These initials also appear on papal coins of 1549–1550 for Ascanio Sforza, papal chamberlain.

A. T. F.: See Travanus, Antonius.

B. or B. C.: See Cotel, Bartolomeo. On later coins of Bologna, "B" stands for Bologna.

B. or B. V.: See Bellagrandi, Tomasso.

Bacceratti, Giovanni, mint master at Fuligno for Leo X, 1513–1515. Signature: B. G.

Balugani, Filippo, die sinker at Bologna, 1774 and later. Signature: PH BAL; F. B.; F. BAL.

Barattani, Francesco, engraver at Bologna for Pius VI (after Balugani; as he signed F. B. F [ECI9] he is sometimes mistaken for the latter).

Bassi, Grammaria, engraver at Bologna, 1692. Signature: B. G.; G. B.

B. C.: See Campi, Bartolomeo.

Bellagrandi, Agostino and Tomasso, of Ravenna, mint masters at Ferrara for Gregory XV and Urban VIII. Agostino signed A. B., Tomasso B., or V. B.

Belli, Valerio, born 1468, died 1546; engraved coins and medals for Clement VII and Paul III.

Beneventi di Spilamberto, Antonio Maria, engraver at Modena from 1738 to 1740.

Bernardi de Castelbolognese, Giovanni, a medal engraver during the first half of the sixteenth century. Worked at Ferrara for Clement VII. Signature: Io; Ioan de Castro Bon; etc.

B. G.: See Bacceratti, Giovanni, and Bassi, Grammaria.

B. H.: See Hameran: Beatrice Hamerani.

Bianchi, F., worked as engraver at Rome during the latter half of the nineteenth century for Pius IX and Leo XIII.

Bonis, Niccolo de, engraver at Rome, 1580–1592, from Pope Sixtus V to Clement VIII.

Bonzagna, Gian Frederigo, called Frederic of Parma or Frederigo Parmense, executed the celebrated St. Bartholomew's Massacre medal. He signed F.; P. F. Parm.; Fede Parm; Fed Parm; or a triangle. He started working at the Rome mint in 1555.

Bonzagna, Giangiacomo, brother of Gian Frederigo; a native of Parma, born 1508, died 1565. He was made a papal engraver for life by Paul III and also worked for Julius III, mostly on medals.

Borgo, Girolamo del, mint master at Rome in the early part of the sixteenth century; was succeeded by Benvenuto Cellini.

Borner, Johann Baptist, a Swiss who settled in Rome, where he became a master of the papal mint; engraved medals for Clement XI and Innocent XII.

Borner, Peter Paul, brother of Johann Baptist Borner. He also settled in Rome and won great renown as an engraver of medals and coins for Popes Alexander VIII, Innocent XII, and Clement XI. His scudi for these popes have the signa-

tures P. B.; P. B. F.; P. P. BORNER F (ECIT) ; P. BFRNER F.;
and P. P. B. F.

B. P.: See Provagli, Bartolomeo.

B. Z.: See Zaccagnini, Bonfiglio.

C.: See Cotel, Bartolomeo.

C. A.: See Garafolini, Carlo Antonio.

Calamanzia, Vincenzo Giovanni, engraver at Macerata, 1587.

Camelio, Vittore, called Gambello, of Venice, chief engraver at
Venice for the doges. Leo X in 1515 appointed him assist-
ant engraver at the Rome mint, under Pier Maria de
Pescia. His signature cannot be found on coins.

Camisano, Francesco, coin engraver at Rome for Clement VII,
1523–1534. Signature F and a crescent on coins of this
pope and a quarter ducat of 1529.

Campi, Bartolomeo, mint master at Pesaro in 1555. Signature:
B. C.

Canobio, Bartolomeo, mint master at Rome for Julius III, 1551–
1554.

Caradosso, Cristoforo, born 1445, died 1527. Engraver for
Julius II, Leo X, and Clement VII. No signed coins.

Casoni, Monsignor S. Andrea, mint master at Rome for Clement XII. His coat of arms appears on coins of that pope.

Casterone, Lorenzo, engraver at Parma at the end of the sixteenth and the beginning of the seventeenth centuries.

Cavallerio, Paolo, engraver at Reggio, 1543–1572.

Cavalli, Gianbattista, engraver at Reggio, 1523.

Cellini, Benvenuto, one of the most famous artists of all time;
equally skilled as sculptor, jeweler, and coin, medal, and
seal engraver. Born in Florence in 1500, Cellini was placed
with a Florentine jeweler at the age of thirteen. He later
worked at Bologna, Pisa, and Rome. Cellini had a colorful
and at times violent career, as is set forth in his famous
autobiography. It was claimed that he once assassinated a
fellow artist through professional pride. While his most
renowned work was performed in other media, he is cred-

ited with some coins, among which are the following, none of which are signed:

Two zecchini of Clement VII, during sack of Rome. Obverse: CLEMENS VII PONT MAX. Reverse: PRO DEO VT ME DILIGERENT—ECCE HOMO ROMA, with figure of Christ.

Two zecchini. Obverse: CLEMENTS VT OMNIS TERRA ADORET ME. Reverse: VNVS SPS ET VNA FIDES ERAT IN EIS, with figures of SS Peter and Paul.

Two julio piece. Obverse: CLEMENS VII PONT MAX. Reverse: QVARE DVBITASTI and figure of St. Peter.

Scudo d'oro for Paul III. Obverse: PAVLVS III PONT MAX. REVERSES S. PAVLVS VAS ELECTIONIS.

Cenli, Girolamo, mint master at Rome, 1550–1554.

Cerbara, Giuseppe, engraver at Rome mint, 1820–1850, for Pius VII, Leo XII, Pius VIII, Gregory XVI, and Pius IX, and sede vacante 1829. Signed G. C.

Cerbara, Niccolo, brother of Giuseppe. Chief engraver at Rome for Pius VIII, Gregory XVI, and Pius IX, and sede vacante 1829, 1830, and 1846. Signed N. C.; NIC. CERBARA; NIC. C.

Cersi, Pandolfa, coin engraver at Ferrara, 1532–1537.

Cesari, Alessandro, mint master at Rome, 1550. Signature: A. C.

Cesarino, F., engraver at Rome, 1670–1680. Signature: F. C. F.

Cesati, Alessandro, called El Greco or Il Grechetto, born in Cyprus about 1538. A fine medal and coin engraver who did medals for Cardinal Alessandro Farnese (later Paul III), and who was employed at the Parma and Rome mints by Julius III, Paul IV, and Pius IV. His medals are signed with the Greek letters for his name.

Christianie, Tommaso de, coin engraver at Rome for Pius IV.

C. L.: See Casterone, Lorenzo, and Corbolini, Lorenzo.

Cocciopuli, Vincenzo, mint master at Parma, 1637–1639. Signed V. C.

Colli, Luigi, papal coiner by contract at Fermo for Pius VI late in 1799. He struck over twenty-five thousand fifty-baiocchi pieces for this pope.

Conti, Antonio, coin engraver at Bologna for Clement XI, 1703–1704.

Corbolini, Lorenzo (Leonardo), engraver at Rome for Alexander VI. Signed C. L. or L. C. F.

Cormano: See Kornmann, Johann Jakob.

Corsolini, Andrea, engraver at Parma, Piacenza, and Ferrara from 1590 to 1594. Signature: A. C.

Cotel, Bartolomeo, engraver for Clement XI at Rome, 1706–1718. Signed B.; B. C.; C.

Cropanese, F., engraver at Rome for Clement XIV. Signed F. C.

E. H.: See Hameran: Ermenigildo Hameranus.

E. L.: See Lelli, Ercole, and Lucenti, Girolamo.

Enzola, Gianfrancesco, called Gianfrancesco Parmense or Parmigiano, engraver at Ferrara, 1472, and at Reggio between 1456 and 1472. While his coins were not signed, some issues of Sixtus IV are ascribed to him.

F.: See Camisano, Francesco.

Faccini, Angelo, engraver at Ferrara mint, 1676.

Facioli or Faciuoli, Girolamo, coin engraver at the Bologna mint at his death in 1573.

F. A. H.: See Hameran: Alberto Hamerani.

Fatinelli, Monsignor, director of Rome mint. His arms appear on scudi of Clement XI, 1713, with a view of the Piazza del Pantheon.

F. B. or F. Bal.: See Balugani, Filippo.

F. B. or F. B. F.: See Barattani, Francesco.

F. D. S. V.: See St. Urbain, Ferdinand de.

F. G.: See Galeotti, Paolo Emilio.

Figino, Girolamo, mint master at Rome about 1550.

F. N.: See Franchini, Nicolo.

F. P.: See Prato, Francesco del.

F. R.: See Franchini, Nicolo, and Rivarole, Agosto.

Fragny, Lorenzo, coin engraver for Gregory XIII. Usually called Lorenzo Parmense. Signed LAV. PAR.; L. P.

Franchini, Niccolo, mint master at Ferrara. His initials appear on some coins of Gregory XV, 1621, and sometimes jointly with those of Agosto Rivarole (q. v.).

Francia, Francesco Raibolini, a famous artist who engraved many papal coins, not identified by his signature. He is credited with the gold zecchino of Julius II: BON. P. IVL A TIRANO LIBERAT.

F. S.: See Sevo, Francesco.

G. A. L.: See Andra, Giovanni.

Galeotti, Giovanni Francesco, mint master at Gubbio for Benedict XIII.

Galeotti, Paolo Emilio, Antonio, Michelangelo, and Guiseppe, mint masters and contractors at Gubbio for Popes Innocent XII and Clement XI. Signed G. G. (Galeotti, Gubbio) and F. G. (Fecit Galeottus).

Gambaro, Pietro de Matteo dal, engraver at Bologna, 1498.

Garafolini, Carlo Antonio, of Viterbo, coin engraver at Viterbo, 1797–1800. Engraver of the sede vacante half scudo of 1797, L'Incendie di Ronciglione.

G. B.: See Bassi, Grammaria.

G. C.: See Cerbara, Giuseppe.

G. F. M.: See Morone, G. F.

G. G.: See Galeotti, Paolo Emilio.

G. H.: See Hameran: Giovanni Hameranus.

Gherardini, Domenico, engraver for Martin V.

Girometti, A., engraver at Rome, Pius IX.

G. M. or G. Mol.: See Mola, Gaspare.

G. P.: See Pignoni, Gaetano.

G. R.: See Rancetti, Giorgi.

G. T.: See Troncio, Guiglielmo.

Guerdini, Michele, mint master at Parma, 1594–1596. Signature: M. G.

Hameran: A famous family of engravers of papal coins and
medals. Johann Andres Hameran, a Bavarian, settled in
Rome during the pontificate of Paul V (1605–1621). He
was an engraver and worked for Paul V, but none of his
coins or medals are signed. He died in 1644, leaving a son:

Alberto Hamerani, born in Rome 1620, died at Rome 1677.
His mother was Margherita Coradini, an Italian. Alberto
was appointed engraver by Clement IX and continued
under Clement X until his death. He signed ALBERTO
HAMERANIS F; ALB HAMERAN; A. H.; ALB HAMERANI;
OPVS HAMERANI; and at times G. G. G. on coins and medals
of Rome and Bologna. He had taken the Italian form of
his name and this form was continued by his family. He
had two children, Anna and Giovanni.

Anna Hamerani, daughter of Alberto, was a good engraver
but executed no coins.

Beatrice Hamerani (or Hameranus), daughter of Giovanni
and granddaughter of Alberto, was born in Rome in 1675
and died there in 1704. She was a medal engraver of fine re-
pute, although only twenty-nine years old when she died.
She executed portrait medals of Innocent XII and cut seals,
and but for her untimely death might have been the most
famous of the family. She assisted her father, Giovanni,
and, according to Cinagli, created the mezzo scudo of Innocent XII, signed B. H. Her signature on medals was BEA
HAMERANI F or B. H.

Gioacchimo Hameranus, grandson of Giovanni and son of Ottone, and the last representative of the family. He was appointed engraver by Pius VI and continued for Pius VII,
and engraved coins for these popes as well as for the Rome
Republic, 1798 and 1799.

Giovanni Hameranus, born in Rome 1649 and died 1705, son
of Alberto. He had two sons, Erminigildo and Ottone, and
one daughter, Beatrice. Giovanni was appointed medalist
after Alberto's death and worked for Clement X and later

for Innocent XI, Alexander VIII, Innocent XII, and Clement XI, signing I. HAMERANVS F; Io HAMERANVS; OPVS HAMERAN; I. H.; I. H. F.; Io HAM; HAM; G. H.; and other forms.

Ermenigildo Hameranus, son of Giovanni, born 1685 and died 1744, succeeded as engraver at the papal mint in 1705 and worked on much of the silver coinage of Clement XI and some of the gold issues; he was also engraver for Innocent XIII and sede vacante 1721. He signed in various ways: HERMENEGILDVS HAMERANVS; HERMEN HAMERANI; E. H.; etc.

Ottone Hameranus, born in Rome 1694 and died 1768, son of Giovanni and father of Gioacchimo. Appointed engraver for Clement XII and continued for Benedict XIV and Clement XIII, and in 1734 was made master of the Rome mint, where he engraved most of the silver coins of Clement XII, Benedict XIV, and Clement XIII. Signed O. H.; OTTO HAMERAN F; and in other ways.

I. I. C. F.: See Kornmann, Johann Jakob.

I. HOR.: See Ortolani, Giovanni.

Io: See Bernardi de Castelbolognese, Giovanni.

I. S.: See Spagnoli, Jacobo.

Kornmann, Johann Jakob, born in Augsburg but moved to Italy and became known as Cormano. Employed at Rome by Urban VIII and Innocent X, 1630–1650. Died in the Inquisition in 1650. His work consisted mostly of medals, which he signed I. I. C. F. (Iohannes Iacob Cormano Fecit) ; OPVS CORMANI—I. I.; or KOREMAN F.

Lelli, Ercole, engraver at Bologna from 1734 to 1766. His signature, E. L., appears on a scudo d'oro of Clement XII, 1736.

Leoni, Leone, famous Italian engraver and painter, born 1509, died 1590. Appointed engraver at Rome in 1537 and was most famous for medals of Paul III. He also engraved coins, none signed. Also worked at Milan and Parma.

Leoni, Ludovico, called Il Podorano, executed coins of Gregory XIII and the jubilee scudo of 1575.

L. S.: See Scajoli, Lelio.

Lucenti, Girolamo, sculptor, medalist, and coin engraver at Rome from 1668 to 1690. Assistant to Gaspare Morone and worked with the Hamerani for Popes Clement X, Innocent XI, and Alexander VIII. Lucenti was knighted by Clement X for his good work, which accounts for his signature: EQ HIER (ONYMUS) LUCENTI; EQ. LUCENTI; and EQVHIER LUCENTI.

Macchiavelli, Antonio, engraver in Bologna for Leo X and Adrian VI, 1520–1523.

Magnani, Antonio di Battista, engraver at Bologna about 1473.

Manfredini, Luigi, engraver at Bologna from 1771 to 1840.

Mazzio, mint master at Rome under Napoleon I. His mark on coins was the Capitoline wolf, which appears also on medals of Benedict XIV.

Menganti, Alessandro, engraver at Bologna, 1573–1585. He cut dies at this mint for Gregory XIII and some coins of Sixtus V.

Mercandetti, Pietro, engraver at Rome, 1767.

Mercandetti, Tomasso, brother of Pietro Mercandetti. Born Rome 1758, died 1821. Engraver at Rome under Pius VI, 1796. Signature: T. M.; T. M. F.; T MERCANDETTI on coins of Pius VI and Pius VII and the Rome Republic. He also signed M. T. in monogram.

Mistruzzi, Aurelio, engraver for Pius XI, sede vacante 1939, and Pius XII at the Italian mint at Rome, where he designed the dies for coins during this period, up to the present time.

Mola, Gaspare, born 1580 at Como. Worked at Florence and was made papal engraver at Rome in 1625, where he succeeded Jacobo Antonio Moro and signed GASP M.; G. M.; G. MOL; GAS MOL. A prolific worker, he is credited with over ninety medals.

Mola, Gaspare Morone, nephew of Gaspare Mola, engraver at Rome, 1637. Succeeded his uncle as chief engraver from 1640 to 1665. He executed many medals and most of the coins of four popes—Urban VIII, Innocent X, Alexander VII, and Clement IX. Most of his coins are unsigned.

Moro, Jacobo Antonio, engraver at Rome for Paul V and Gregory XV. He was succeeded by Gaspare Mola. He executed coins of Paul V, not signed. His signature on medals is sometimes confused with that of Gaspare Morone Mola.

Morone, G. F., die sinker at Rome about 1628. Signature: G. F. M.

Motti, M. A., die cutter for coins of Pius XI, sede vacante 1939, and Pius XII.

M. P.: See Parmensis, Marmetta.

M. T.: See Mercandetti, Tomasso.

N. C.: See Cerbara, Niccolo.

N. F.: See Franchini, Niccolo.

O. H.: See Hameran: Ottone Hameranus.

Orsini, Emeliano, engraver at Fuligno about 1465 to 1487. His coins for Paul II include a four zecchini piece, with the motto MODICE FIDEI QVARE DVBITASTI, and the famous double zecchino of this pope.

Ortolani, Giovanni, engraver at Rome during the latter half of the seventeenth century. Signed I. HOR.; Io Ho.

Ortolani, Stefano, engraver; brother of Giovanni Ortolani.

Parmensis, Lorenzo, engraver at Rome in the early seventeenth century. Signed LAV. P. or L. PAR.

Parmensis, Marmetta (Lodovico), engraver at Rome, 1550.

Passamonti, S., chief engraver at Rome in the nineteenth century for Pius VII.

P. B., P. B. F., or P. P. B. F.: See Borner, Peter Paul.

Perpenti, Andronica, engraver at Fermo from 1797 to 1799 for Pius VI. Signature: A. P. or A. P. P.

Pesci, Silvestro, mint master at Parma, 1658–1660. Signed S. P.

Pignoni, Gaetano, engraver at Bologna, 1786–1795.

Pistrucci, Benedetto, born 1784, died at London 1855. Chief engraver for Papal States, 1839, but is most famous for his work at the London mint, where he made the pattern coins for King George IV.

Poggini, Domenico, engraved coins for Sixtus V, not signed.

Prato, Francesco del, engraver at Rome, 1562. Signed F. P.

Provagli, Bartolomeo, mint master at Bologna, 1653–1671, where he made coins for Alexander VII and Clement X. Signature: B. P.

Provagli, Orazio, father of Bartlomeo Provagli; engraved coins for Urban VIII and Innocent X at Bologna.

P. T. or P. T. F.: See Todolini, Petronio.

Rancetti, Giorgi, worked for the Medici and at Rome, where he engraved coins for Clement VIII. Many medals and coins were engraved by him at Rome between 1594 and 1610. His signature on medals was GIOR RAN, GIORG R., and G. R.

Rivarole, Agosto, mint master at Parma, 1614–1617, and at Ferrara, 1619. His initials, A. R., appear on some coins at Ferrara; also jointly with those of Niccolo Franchini on Ferrarese coins of Gregory XV (F. R.: Franchini and Rivarole).

Rossi, Giovanni Antonio de, engraved coins for Pius IV, Pius V, and Gregory XIII.

S.: See Siliprandi, Giuseppe.

Scajoli, Lelio, mint master at Parma, 1580–1604. Signature: L. S.

Segni, Antonio, mint master at Fuligno, 1500–1516. His signature, A. S., appears on julios of Julius II.

Sevo, Francesco, engraver at Rome in the eighteenth century. Signature: F. S.

Siliprandi, Giuseppe, engraver at Parma, 1784–1787. Signature: S.

S. P.: See Pesci, Silvestro.

Spagnoli, Jacobo, mint master at Ferrara, whose initials, I. S., sometimes in monogram form, are on coins issued for Innocent X.

S. T.: See Tiseo, Salvatino.

St. Urbain, Claude August, engraver at Rome, 1725–1737.

St. Urbain, Ferdinand de, a Frenchman who was appointed engraver at Bologna in 1673 and at Rome in 1683. Many scudi show his initials, F. D. S. V. or S. V. Father of Claude August St. Urbain.

S. V.: See St. Urbain, Ferdinand de.

Tedesco, Pietro, chief engraver at Bologna for Clement X, 1675.

Tiseo, Salvatino, mint master at Parma, 1673–1679. Signed S. T.

T. M. F.: See Mercandetti, Tomasso.

Todolini, Petronio, engraver at Bologna, 1775–1800, where he made coins of Pius VI signed P. TAD., P. T., or P. T. F (ecit).

Travanus, Antonius, engraver at Rome mint from 1684 to 1692. His initials, A. T. F (ecit), are on the obverse side of gold scudi of Alexander VIII, 1689, and others. Antonius Travanus was the son of Giachomo Francesca Travanus, and was born in Rome in 1654.

Troncio, Guglielmo, of Pisa, administrator of the papal mint at Rome from 1578 to 1598. His coins for Clement VIII are signed G. T. or G+T or ⚲ .

V. C.: See Cocciopuli, Vincenzo.

Zaccagnini, Bonfiglio, engraver at Rome for Pius IX. His signature, B. Z., is found on gold scudi of 1853 and later years and on the quattrini of 1851 to 1854.

Bibliography

Ambrosoli, Solone, *Atlante numismatico. italiano*, U. Hoepli, Milan, 1906.

Bellini, Vincenzo, *Delle monete di Ferrara*, Ferrara, 1761.

Beneven, Jean Michel, *De l'état ecclésiastique monnoies de Rome*, 2 vols., 1787.

Berni, Giulio, *Le monete e le medaglie degli anni santi*, Caserta–E. E. Marino, 1925.

Bonanni, Philippo, *Numismatica pontificum Romanorum qua tempore Martino V*, 2 vols., 1698.

Casa Savoia (Vittorio Emanuele III, King of Italy), *Corpus nummorum Italicorum*, Vols. 1–16, 1910–1936, Tipografia della R. Accademia de Lincei (U. Hoepli), Rome.

Catholic Encyclopedia.

Cinagli, Angelo, *Le monete de' papi*, 1848.

Crespellani, Arsenio, *La zecca di Modena*, Modena, 1884.

Mann, Rt. Rev. Horace K., *The Lives of the Popes in the Middle Ages*, Kegan Paul, Trench, Trubner & Co., Ltd., London, and B. Herder Book Co., St. Louis, Mo.

Orsini, Ignazio, *Monete della republica e del granducato di Tuscano*, Florence, 1760.

Promis, D., *Monete e medaglie italiane,* Turin, 1873.

Serafini, Camillo, *Le monete e le bolle plumbee pontificie del medagliere vaticano*, Milan, 1910.

Prices

With the exception of twentieth-century papal coins, values of which are more or less standard, prices are generally fixed by those realized at dealers' auctions.

Rare gold coins are sold at higher prices, according to rarity, followed by silver coins of extreme rarity. Silver scudi or five lire pieces of crown or dollar size range in price from $2.50 or $3.00 for those of the later popes, Pius VI, Pius VII, Leo XII, and Gregory XVI, to $8.50 and as high as $20.00 for scudi of the earlier popes. Scarcity governs the cost of earlier small silver coins; for example, the julio of Marcellus II (Plate I, No. 2) sells for $8.50 in fine condition. Since this pope reigned only twenty-two days his coins are all scarce. Another rarity is the pattern five lire of Leo XIII, which lists for $15.00.

All papal coins are not costly. The profuse copper issues, and small silver coins of the last half of the seventeenth and all of the eighteenth centuries in very fine condition can all be secured at less than $1.00 each.

Prices given herein for coins other than those of the twentieth century are for coins in very fine condition. Uncirculated coins would be priced at approximately 25 per cent higher; those in only fine condition approximately 20 per cent lower.

Prices of coins shown in the plates:

Plate I			Plate II		
No.	1—$	2.50	No.	7—$	2.50
"	2—	8.50	"	8—	1.00
"	3—	1.50	"	9—	1.50
"	4—	1.50	"	10—	2.00
"	5—	2.00	"	11—	8.50
"	6—	1.00	"	12—	8.50

Plate III

    No. 13—$ 7.50
     "   14— 8.50
     "   15— 1.50
     "   16— 2.50
     "   17— 2.00
     "   18— 1.25

Plate IV

    No. 19—$ 2.00
     "   20— 15.00
     "   21— 16.50

Plate V

    No. 22— 12.50
     "   23— 9.00
     "   24— 7.00
     "   25—   .75

Plate VI

    No. 26— 6.00
     "   27— 1.00
     "   28— 12.50
     "   29— 1.00
     "   30— 5.00

Plate VII

    No. 31— 7.50
     "   32— 3.00
     "   33— 4.50
     "   34— 3.50

Plate VIII

    No. 35— 9.50
     "   36— 9.00
     "   37— 12.50

Plate IX

    No. 38— 7.50
     "   39—   .75
     "   40— 16.50
     "   41— 12.50
     "   42— 2.50

Plate X

    No. 43— 4.50
     "   44— 9.50
     "   45— 1.00
     "   46— 6.50
     "   47— 1.00

Plate XI

    No. 48— 3.50
     "   49— 7.50
     "   50— 15.00
     "   51— 2.00
     "   52— 1.25

Plate XII

    No. 53— 4.50
     "   54— 1.50
     "   55— 5.00
     "   56— 2.00
     "   57— 18.00
     "   58—   .75
     "   59— 3.00

Plate XIII

No. 60—$ .85
"   61— 12.00
"   62—   .75
"   63—   .35
"   64—   .35
"   65—   .25

Plate XIV

No. 66—$ .45
"   67—   1.00
"   68—   .50
"   69—   1.50
"   70—   3.00
"   71—   4.50

Plate XV

No. 72—   3.50
"   73—   7.50
"   74—   2.50
"   75—   2.50
"   76—   .35
"   77—   .65

Plate XVI

No. 78—   1.50
"   79— 25.00
"   80—   2.00
"   81—   1.50
"   82—   .50
"   83—   .35
"   84—   .25

Index to Plates

161

10. Urban VIII, 1623–1644.
Testone, silver, jubilee issue 1625.
Obverse: Arms; Vrbanvs VIII Pon Max A. III.
Reverse: Porta Sancta with Veronica's veil showing head of Christ; Qvi Ingreditvr Sine Macvla. Ro—ma separated by Holy Door; Date 16—25 in exergue.

11. Scudo, silver.
Obverse: Bust right; Vrbanvs VIII Pont. Max. An XII, under bust; under shoulder Gasp. Mol and mint director's mark (Gaspare Mola, engraver).
Reverse: Archangel Michael with sword and shield casting Satan into Hell; Vivit Devs; in exergue Ro—ma, separated by arms.

12. Scudo, silver.
Obverse: Bust right; Vrbanvs VIII Pon. Max. A XXI; date under bust; G. M. under shoulder.
Reverse: SS Peter and Paul under radiant dove (Holy Spirit); Roma separated by arms, under line, all enclosed in wreath.

PLATE III.

13. Innocent X, 1644–1650.
Scudo, silver.
Obverse: Bust right; Innocent (iv)s. Pont Max Anno XVII; small 1650.
Reverse: Holy door showing Veronica's veil and Ro—ma separated by door, all in wreath; Anno Ivbilei MDCL.

14. Alexander VII, 1655–1667.
Obverse: Arms surmounted by reclining genei; Alex VII Pont Max Romæ.
Reverse: St. Thomas of Villanova giving alms to crippled beggar; Dispersit Dedit Pavperibvs I. E. M. I. S. S.

15. Sede vacante 1669.
Carlino, silver.
Obverse: Arms of Camerlingo Cardinal Emilio Altieri; Sede Vacante MDCLXIX.
Reverse: Radiant dove (Holy Ghost) over flames; Illvxit Illvcescat Adhvc.

16. Clement X, 1670–1676.
Two grossi silver.
Obverse: Bust right; Clemens X Pont Max.
Reverse: St. Paul with sword; S. Pavlvs Apostolvs.

17. Testone, silver.
Obverse: Same as preceding, except A. I, and date in exergue MDCLXX.
Reverse: St. Peter crowned by an angel; Colles Flvent Mel de Petra; in exergue S. Petrvs—M (St. Peter—Martyr).

18. Grosso, silver, jubilee year.
Obverse: Bust right.
Reverse: Holy door closed; Apervit et Clavsit. In exergue 1675.

PLATE IV.

19. Testone, silver, jubilee year 1675.
Obverse: Arms; Clemens X Pont Max.
Reverse: Holy door open with cardinals and guards; Dedi Coram (Te Ostivm) Apertvm.

20. Scudo, silver, jubilee year.

Obverse: Bust right; CLEMENS X PONT MAX AN IVB. EQ. HIER. LVCENTI (engraver) under bust.

Reverse: Holy Door with figures of SS Peter and Paul; CLAVSIS FORIBVS VENIET ET DABIT PACEM—MDCLXXV (1675); arms of Mgr. Renato Imperiali.

21. Scudo, silver, jubilee year.

Obverse: Bust right; same inscription as No. 20; EQ. HIER. LVCENTI under bust.

Reverse: Holy Door being opened, soldiers and people watching; on portico DILIGIT DNVS PORTAS SION; in exergue MDCL—XXV separated by arms of Mgr. Giovanni Battista Costaguti.

PLATE V.

22. Innocent XI, 1676–1689.

Scudo, silver.

Obverse: Bust right; INNOCEN. XI PONT. MAX. AN. I. HAMERANVS F. (engraver) under bust.

Reverse: St. Matthew seated on cloud writing in book at dictation of an angel; SANCTVS MATTHÆVS APOSTOLVS; in exergue arms of Mgr. Raggi.

23. Scudo, silver.

Obverse: Bust right; INNOCEN. XI PONT. MAX. AN. II. I. HAMERANVS under bust.

Reverse: View of St. Peter's; PORTÆ INFERI NON PRÆVALEBVNT; I. and H. to left and right of base of church; in exergue RO—MÆ separated by arms of Mgr. Raggi.

24. Scudo, silver.

Obverse: Bust right; INNOCEN. XI PONT MAX A. VIII Io. HAMERANVS F. (Giovanni Hameranus, engraver).

Reverse: DEXTERA TVA DOMINE PERCVSSIT INIMICVM in palm wreath.

25. Grosso, silver.

Obverse: Arms.

Reverse: NOCET MINVS—1685 in frame.

PLATE VI.

26. Undated scudo, silver.

Obverse: Arms; INNOCENTIVS XI PONT. MAX.

Reverse: NON | PRODERVNT | IN DIE | VLTIONIS in garland of laurel.

27. Sede vacante 1689.

Grosso, silver.

Obverse: Arms of Cardinal Camerlingo Paluzzo Altieri surmounted by umbrella and keys; SEDE VACANTE MDCLXXXIX.

Reverse: Dove representing Holy Ghost; VBI VVLT SPIRAT; RO—MA separated by arms of Mgr. d'Aste.

28. Alexander VIII, 1689–1691.

Scudo, silver, first year.

Obverse: Bust right; HAMERANVS F. under bust; ALEXANDER VIII PONT. MAX. A. I.

Reverse: Figure wearing tiara representing the Church facing left holding church and staff with military insignia; LEGIONE AD BELLVM SACRVM

INSTRVCTA; in exergue date (1690) in decorative style CIƆIƆ—CXC separated by arms of Mgr. Patrizi.

29. Half grosso, silver.
Obverse: Arms; ALEXANDER VIII PONT. M.
Reverse: SACROS | BASILIC | LATERAN | POSSESS | 1689 in decorative frame. This money was distributed to the poor on the occasion of the pope's taking possession of the Basilica October 23, 1689. This was one of the pope's first official duties, the money distributed usually being in baser metal.

30. Testone, silver.
Obverse: Bust right; ALEXAN. VIII PONT. M. A. I. HAMERANVS under bust.
Reverse: Two oxen in field of wheat; RE. FRVMENTARIA RESTITVTA; Date (1690) in decorative style CIƆIƆ—CXC separated by arms of Mgr. Patrizi.

PLATE VII.

31. Innocent XII, 1691–1700.
Scudo, silver.
Obverse: Bust right; HAMERANVS under bust; INNOCEN. XII PONT. MAX. A. II.
Reverse: Archangel Michael casting Lucifer into Hell; DEVS PACIS CONTERET SATANAM; 1692 in minute figures under arms of Mgr. Farsetti.

32. Testone, silver.
Obverse: Arms; INNOCEN. XII PONT. M. A. IIII.
Reverse: Figure representing abundance distributing money from a cornucopia; EGENO ET PAVPERI; in exergue 1694; to right arms of Mgr. Farsetti.

33. Half scudo, silver.
Obverse: Bust right; S. V. (St. Urbain, engraver) under bust; INNOCEN. XII PON. M. AN. VI.
Reverse: The Pope praying before dove representing Holy Ghost. FIAT PAX IN VIRTVTE TVA; in exergue S. V. and arms of Mgr. Farsetti.

34. Half scudo, silver.
Obverse: Bust right; S. V. in exergue; INNO. XII P. M. AN. VII.
Reverse: Noah's arm resting on mountain; FACTVS EST IN PACE LOCVS EIVS; in exergue S. V. and arms of Mgr. Farsetti.

PLATE VIII.

35. Scudo, silver.
Obverse: Bust right; INNOCEN XII PONT. MAX. ANN. VI; S. V. under bust.
Reverse: Peace council or consistory; dove in cloud representing Holy Ghost; PACEM LOQUETUR GENTIBUS; to left above line FERD. DE S. V.; in exergue arms of Mgr. Farsetti.

36. Scudo, silver.
Obverse: Bust right; INNOCEN. XII P. M. AN. VIII; S. VRBA. OP in exergue.
Reverse: St. Peter with keys preaching to kneeling people; GRATIA VOBIS ET PAX MVLTIPLICETVR; in exergue large S. V.—OP. (St. Urbain—Opus); 16—98 separated by arms of Mgr. Farsetti.

37. Scudo, silver.
Obverse: Bust right; INNOCEN. XII PONT. MAX. A. IX; S. V. under bust.
Reverse: Trumpeting angels at each side of Holy Door; ANNO IVBILEI MDCC; arms of Mgr. Anguisciola.

PLATE XI.

48. Half scudo, silver.
   Obverse: Bust left; CLEMENS XI P. M. AN. XI.
   Reverse: Front and side view of the Pantheon, S. Maria Rotonda; DILEXI DE
   COREM DOMVS TVÆ; in exergue E—H (Ermenigildo Hameranus, engraver)
   separated by arms of Mgr. Altieri.

49. Scudo, silver.
   Obverse: Arms; CLEMENS XI. P. M. AN. XIII.
   Reverse: View of the obelisk and fountain, Plaza della Rotonda; FONTIS ET
   FORI ORNAMEN; in exergue E H and arms of Mgr. Fattinelli.

50. Benedict XIII, 1724–1730.
   Zecchino, gold.
   Obverse: Figure representing Religion, with keys and church; BEN. XIII
   P. MAX.
   Reverse: A rose; ZECCHINO ROMANO; in exergue 1729.

51. Clement XII, 1730–1740.
   Half scudo, silver.
   Obverse: Arms; CLEMENS XII PONT. M. A. IV.
   Reverse: FRVSTRA | VIGILAT | QVI | CVSTODIT; arms of Mgr. Casoni in palm
   spray.

52. Clement XIII, 1758–1769.
   Julio, silver.
   Obverse: Arms; CLEMENS XIII PON. M. AN. II.
   Reverse: Figure representing Religion with church and keys; SVPRA FIRMAM
   PETRAM 1759; arms of Mgr. de Vecchis.

PLATE XII.

53. Clement XII, 1730–1740.
   Half scudo, silver.
   Obverse: Bust right; CLEMENS XII P. M. A. VII.
   Reverse: Front view of Church of St. John Fiorentini; DECVS PATRIÆ. In
   exergue MDCC—XXXVI separated by arms of Mgr. Casoni; O. H. (Ottone
   Hameranus, engraver).

54. Testone, silver.
   Obverse: Bust right; CLEMENS XII P. M. AN. VII.
   Reverse: Seated figure, female, representing Commerce holding wheel; COM-
   MODITAS VIARVM REDVX. In exergue date, MDCC—XXXVI; arms of Mgr.
   Casoni, director of Rome mint.

55. Benedict XIV, 1740–1758.
   Quartino, gold.
   Obverse: Tiara and keys; BEN | XIV above palm spray.
   Reverse: St. Peter, head facing right, with nimbus; SAN PETRVS.

56. Testone, silver.
   Obverse: Bust right; BEN XIV PON. MAX. VII.
   Reverse: Religion seated in cloud holding church and keys; MDCC—LVI.

57. Zecchino, gold.
   Obverse: Figure representing Religion holding keys and church; BEN. XIV.
   P. M. A. XII. 1752.

Reverse: Arms surmounted by dove representing Holy Ghost; REPENTE DE COELO.

58. Grosso, silver.
 Obverse: Arms; BENED XIV PON. MAX. VII.
 Reverse: The Blessed Virgin; TOTA PVLCHRA ES.
59. Scudo, silver.
 Obverse: Bust right; BENED XIV PONT. MAX. AN. XIV; under bust O. HAMERANI.
 Reverse: Figure representing Religion holding keys and church. MDCC—LIII.

PLATE XIII.

60. Sede vacante 1769.
 One-fifth scudo, or two julii, silver.
 Obverse: Arms of Cardinal Camerlingo Carlo Rezzonico; SEDE VACANTE MDCCLXIX.
 Reverse: Holy Ghost in form of a dove; VENI SANCTE SPIRITVS; small QVINTO DI SCV.
61. Pius VI, 1775–1799.
 Zecchino, gold, issued at Bologna.
 Obverse: Arms; PIVS VI PONT. M. and date 17—78.
 Reverse: St. Petronius; BONONIA PATRONVS; arms of the city of Bologna and Cardinal Ignazio Boncompagni.
62. Twenty paoli, silver, issued at Bologna.
 Obverse: Arms; PIVS VI PONT. M.
 Reverse: Lion with banner, part of arms of city of Bologna; BONON. DOCET 1778; denomination 20 beneath lion.
63. Two baiocchi, copper, Perugia mint.
 Obverse: Arms; PIVS SEXTVS PON. M. A. XXI.
 Reverse: Denomination DVE | BAIOCCHI and date 1795 in beaded circle; PERVSIA AVGVSTA between inner and outer circle.
64. Two and one-half baiocchi, copper, Gubbio mint.
 Obverse: St. Peter, bust facing left, holding keys; APOSTOLORUM PRINCEPS; all in circle.
 Reverse: BAIOCCHI | DVE E MEZZO | GVBBIO | 1795.
65. One baiocco, copper, Gubbio mint.
 Obverse: Arms; PIVS SEXTVS PON. MAX. VIII.
 Reverse: VN | BAIOCCO | GVBBIO in circle of flowers.

PLATE XIV.

66. Two baiocchi, copper, Fuligno mint.
 Obverse: Arms; PIVS SEXTVS. PON. M. A. XXI.
 Reverse: DVE | BAIOCCHI | DI | FVLIGNO in flowered circle.
67. Grosso, silver.
 Obverse: Arms; PIVS VII P. M. A. XVII.
 Reverse: PAVPERI | PORRIGE | MANVM above line; MDCCCXVI and mint mark B, with star on either side in exergue; all enclosed in flowered border.

68. Pius VII, 1800–1823.
    Baiocco, copper.
    Obverse: Arms; Sacrosan. Basilicæ Lateranen. Possess; in exergue Baiocco;
    all enclosed in circle.
    Reverse: Pivs | Septimvs | Pontifex Maximvs; under line MDCCCI and three
    Negro heads from pope's arms.
69. Twenty baiocchi, silver.
    Obverse: Arms; Pivs VII. P. M. A. XVII.; small M̃, mark of engraver, To-
    masso Mercandetti.
    Reverse: Religion holding keys and church; Avxilivm de Sancto; 1816;
    Bologna mint mark, B.
70. Scudo, silver.
    Obverse: Arms; Pivs VII Pon. M. A. XVI.
    Reverse: Religion seated on cloud with keys and church; Avxilivm de Sancto;
    1815. Pasinati (engraver) and arms of Mgr. Lante in exergue.
71. Leo XII, 1823–1829.
    Scudo, silver.
    Obverse: Bust left; Leo XII Pon. Max. Anno III; beneath bust G. Cerbara
    F. (engraver).
    Reverse: Figure representing Religion holding cross, pointing to church;
    above, a triangle and Divine Eye representing Blessed Trinity; Avxilivm
    de Sancto; in exergue Cerbara, B (Bologna mint), and date 1825.

PLATE XV.

72. Sede vacante 1829.
    Scudo, silver, proof.
    Obverse: Arms of Cardinal Camerlingo Pier Francesco Galleffi; Sede Vacante
    MDCCCXXIX.
    Reverse: Seated figure representing Religion holding cross and pointing to
    church; Avxilivm de Sancto; R, Rome mint mark; G. C. (G. Cerbara, en-
    graver) in monogram.
73. Pius VIII, 1829–1830.
    Scudo, silver, proof.
    Obverse: Bust right; Pivs VIII Pont. Max. Anno I 1830; in exergue C. Voigt
    (engraver).
    Reverse: Full figures SS Peter and Paul; Isti Svnt Patres Tvi Veriqve
    Pastores; below line, mint mark B.
74. Gregory XVI, 1831–1846.
    Fifty baiocchi, silver, proof.
    Obverse: Bust right; Gregorivs XVI Pont. Max. A. II; in exergue 1832 and
    N. Cerbara (engraver).
    Reverse: St. Romuald praying in desert before rock holding skull, staff resting
    on rock; S. Romvaldvs Ab. Camal; in exergue denomination and mint
    mark Bai. R. 50.
75. Scudo, silver, proof.
    Obverse: Bust left; Gregorivs XVI Pon. Max. A. III; in exergue Nic. Cerbara
    (engraver) and date 1833.
    Reverse: Presentation of the child Jesus in the temple; Lvmen ad Revela-
    tionem Gentivm; in exergue Roma.

76. Pius IX, 1846–1878.
    Half baiocco, copper.
    Obverse: Arms; Pivs IX Pon Max An IIII.
    Reverse: Mezzo | Baiocco | 1849 above line; mint mark R below line; all in floral circle.
77. One soldo, silver.
    Obverse: Bust left in circle; Pivs IX Pont. Max. Ann. XXI 1867.
    Reverse: 1 Soldo R in circle; Stato Pontificio 5 Cent.

PLATE XVI.

78. Pius XI, 1922–1939.
    Ten lire, silver.
    Obverse: Bust left; Pivs XI Pont. Max A XV; Mistrvzzi (engraver) in minute letters in exergue.
    Reverse: Madonna on throne; Stato della Citta del Vaticano; denomination L.—10 separated by throne; 19—36 separated by base of throne; Regina Pacis on base of throne.
79. One hundred lire, gold.
    Obverse: Bust right; Pivs XI Pont. Max. Anno XV.
    Reverse: Full-length figure of Christ, child kneeling with flowers; Stato della Citta del Vaticano; Denomination Lire—100; date 1936 in exergue.
80. Sede vacante 1939.
    Obverse: Arms of Cardinal Camerlingo Eugenio Pacelli; Sede Vacante MCMXXXIX.
    Reverse: Dove representing Holy Ghost; Infvnde Amorem Cordibvs; Stato della Citta del Vaticano; L. 10; in minute letters Mistrvzzi (engraver).
81. Pius XII, 1939.
    Two lire, nickel.
    Obverse: Arms; Pivs XII Pontifex Maximvs A. I.
    Reverse: Good shepherd; Stato della Citta del Vaticano; L. 2.
82. One lire, nickel.
    Obverse: Arms; Pivs XII Pontifex Maximvs A. I.
    Reverse: Blessed Virgin; Stato della Citta del Vaticano; Lire 1; in minute letters Mistrvzzi (engraver) and Motti, Inc. (die cutter).
83. Fifty centesimi, nickel.
    Obverse: Arms; Pivs XII Pontifex Maximvs A. I. 19—39.
    Reverse: Archangel Michael; Stato della Citta del Vaticano C. 50; in exergue Mistrvzzi and A. Motti, Inc.
84. Twenty centesimi, copper.
    Obverse: Arms; Pivs XII Pontifex Maximvs A. I.
    Reverse: St. Peter facing left; Stato della Citta del Vaticano; C. 10; Mistrvzzi and A. Motti, Inc., in minute letters.

PLATE I

PLATE II

PLATE III

PLATE IV

PLATE V

PLATE VI

PLATE VII

35

36

37

PLATE VIII

38   39   38

40

41

42   39   42

PLATE IX

43   45   43

44

46

45

47   47

PLATE X

PLATE XI

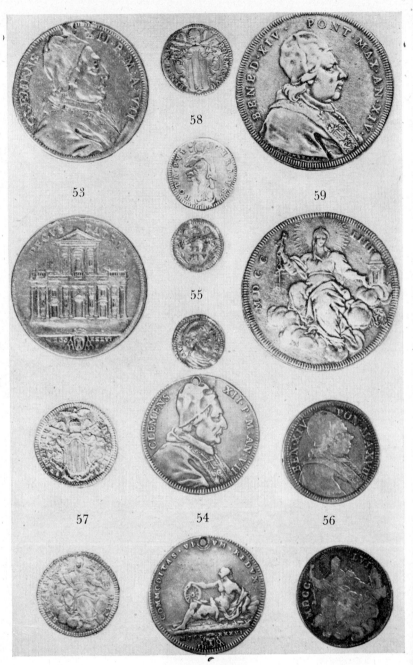

58

53

59

55

57

54

56

PLATE XII

60   61   60

62   62

63   64   63

65   65

PLATE XIII

70 67 70

68

66 66

71

69 67 69

PLATE XIV

72 74 72

73 73

75 76 75

77 77

PLATE XV

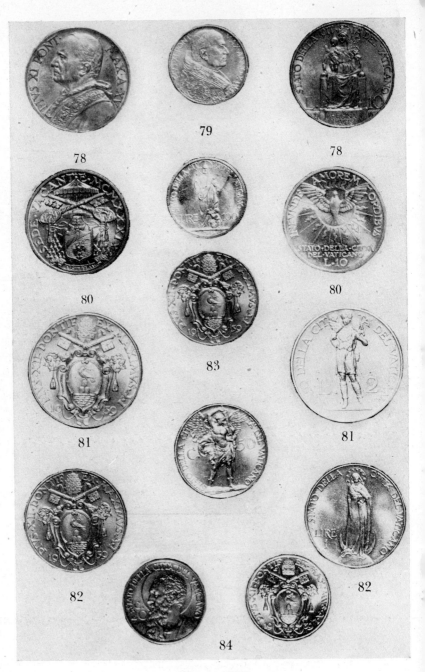

78

79

78

80

80

83

81

81

82

82

84

PLATE XVI